1

Nine Lives of Magic: Working with Your Feline Familiar

Part 1: The History and Mystery of Cats in Magick

For millennia, cats have captivated us with their grace, independence, and enigmatic presence. In ancient Egypt, they were revered as deities, guardians of the home, and symbols of good luck. Across cultures, folklore paints them as lucky companions, protectors from the unseen, and even messengers from the spirit world. But in the realm of witchcraft, a deeper connection exists – the bond between witch and familiar, often taking the form of a cherished feline friend.

This book invites you to explore the fascinating world of cat magick. Explore the history and mystery of cats in magical practices, from their divine origins in ancient Egypt to their enduring association with witchcraft. Discover how your feline companion can become a trusted partner in your magical journey, offering protection, intuition, and a unique connection to the unseen.

Within these pages, you'll find practical exercises and rituals to strengthen your bond with your cat, incorporate cat-inspired elements into your spells, and create a magical home that welcomes both of you. Whether you're a seasoned witch or just beginning to explore the power of intuition and connection, 'Nine Lives of Magic' will guide you on a journey of self-discovery and feline companionship.

Are you ready to unlock the nine lives of magic within your cat and yourself? Let the purr-fect adventure begin!

Chapter 1: Bastet and the Feline Deities of Egypt

Cats have captivated humanity for millennia, their grace, independence, and enigmatic presence weaving a spell across cultures. From revered companions in ancient Egypt to cherished house pets today, these felines have held a unique place in our hearts and imaginations. Across civilizations, humans have revered cats. But in ancient Egypt, the bond reached a new level of intensity.

Cats weren't simply companions but were elevated to the celestial realm, becoming gods and goddesses. The ancient Egyptians boasted a vibrant pantheon brimming with deities, many adorned with the features of various animals. Among these, cat goddesses reigned supreme, capturing the hearts and imaginations of the people.

Step back in time to the Old Kingdom of Egypt (c. 2686-2181 BCE). Here, the seeds of feline reverence were sown. This chapter explores the fascinating world of Egyptian cat deities, with a special focus on Bastet. Originally envisioned as a powerful lioness, a symbol of protection and solar energy, Bastet's image would evolve over the centuries. Centuries flowed by, and Bastet's depiction underwent a fascinating shift. By the New Kingdom (c. 1550-1069 BCE), her fierce lioness form softened.

Now, she was most often seen as a beautiful woman with a cat's head, embodying not just protection, but also nurturing qualities like love, fertility, and domesticity. By exploring the myths and symbolism surrounding Bastet, Sekhmet, Mafdet, and other cat deities, we embark on a journey that unlocks the profound respect Egyptians held for these creatures. Through their captivating stories and symbolism surrounding these cat gods and goddesses, we gain a window into the intricate bond between humans and felines, a connection that continues to echo across time.

Feline Guardians of the Nile

The Egyptians and cats – a bond forged in time! Our understanding suggests this connection stretches back millennia, with evidence placing its origins around 2000 BCE. While the exact nature of these early interactions remains shrouded in some mystery, practicality likely played a significant role. Evidence suggests that around 2000 BCE, Egyptians began to view cats, with their keen eyesight and unmatched hunting prowess, as invaluable allies in the fight against a constant threat: rodents.

Unlike any guard dog, the cat possessed a unique set of skills perfectly suited to protecting Egypt's food supply. Their silent movements and exceptional eyesight allowed them to patrol homes and granaries with unmatched efficiency. These feline guardians tirelessly hunted and subdued the rodent menace, ensuring precious food stores remained safe from destruction. This vital role undoubtedly cemented the cat's place as a revered and admired creature in the eyes of the Egyptians.

But the Egyptian-feline connection went far deeper than just a practical partnership. Cats, with their ability to thrive in the unseen realm of night, possessed a world beyond the reach of human sight. Their exceptional senses and nocturnal habits imbued them with an aura of mystery.
The Egyptians saw cats not just with their eyes, but with their hearts. They believed these creatures possessed an extra sense, a feline sixth sense that allowed them to navigate the unseen.

When shadows danced and secrets whispered, cats were seen as vigilant guardians, their graceful movements as a shield against unseen dangers and malevolent spirits that might threaten the living. The belief in cats as mystical guardians played a significant role in the development of Egyptian mythology. This reverence for felines led to the creation of several powerful deities with feline forms. These deities were seen as protectors and embodied the concept of divine power.

The Rise of the Feline Divine

The Egyptians' appreciation for cats transcended their usefulness as pest control. Over millennia, as their religion evolved, the Egyptians elevated these creatures to the highest echelons of their religion, transforming them into revered deities. As we mentioned, Bastet was a major cat deity, appearing on tons of statues, amulets, and paintings. You could see her depicted as a woman with a cat head or just a cool black cat.

Bastet's origins may be traced back to the fearsome lion goddess, Sekhmet, a stark contrast to the gentler Bastet. Channeling the sun god Ra's dual nature, Sekhmet embodied both the destructive might of the sun and served as a powerful protector of the pharaohs. A shift occurred in the Egyptian view of felines. The once-feared power of Sekhmet gave way to a newfound appreciation for their grace, cunning, and nurturing nature.

This change led to the rise of Bastet, a deity embodying the gentler aspects of the feline spirit, a stark contrast to the ferocious Sekhmet. Unlike the fearsome Sekhmet, Bastet's influence transcended the fierce aspects of felines. She found herself linked to benevolent goddesses like Isis and Mut, taking on protective roles for homes, women, and children. Bastet even came to symbolize the nurturing warmth of the sun, a complete shift from the destructive power previously associated with lion goddesses.

Bastet: The Many Faces of the Cat Goddess

In the mighty pantheon of Egyptian deities, Bastet reigned supreme as the protector of the home and family. Egyptians revered her as a fierce guardian, warding off illness, malevolent spirits, and misfortune that threatened their loved ones. This protective role likely stemmed from the Egyptians' keen observation of cats.

Felines, with their sharp senses and unwavering alertness, were seen as vigilant guardians, ever watchful against potential threats that could disrupt the peace and safety of the home. Bastet's link to motherhood and fertility further cemented her role as a nurturing deity. The Egyptians, deeply connected to the natural world, saw the abundant litters of cats as a manifestation of Bastet's blessings, mirroring the cyclical renewal present in nature.

Bastet's influence transcended the earthly realm, reaching into the celestial sphere. The Egyptians revered the moon, associating it with cyclical renewal and a gentle, nurturing energy. In turn, Bastet became a celestial reflection of the moon's qualities. Just as the moon's phases ensured the constant ebb and flow of life, Bastet mirrored this cycle, offering comfort and security to her devotees.

Depictions and Symbolism

The Egyptians' enduring love for Bastet is beautifully captured in the abundance of her artistic representations. These depictions, ranging from majestic statues to personal amulets, served not only as a constant reminder of her presence but also fostered a deep emotional connection between the people and their beloved feline goddess. From towering statues guarding temple entrances to delicate amulets nestled against the skin for protection, Bastet's image permeated every aspect of life. Common depictions showcase her holding a sistrum, a sacred rattle used in religious ceremonies. This instrument symbolized music and joy, reflecting Bastet's association with both fierce protection and life's pleasures.

Another iconic image portrays her cradling a basket overflowing with playful kittens. This endearing scene not only highlights Bastet's connection to motherhood and fertility but also emphasizes the abundance Egyptians believed she bestowed upon their families. Perhaps the most powerful image depicts Bastet nursing a pharaoh. This scene transcends mere nourishment, symbolizing Bastet's role as a protector and provider, ensuring the health and well-being of not just families, but the entire nation.

Examining these artistic representations unveils a treasure trove of symbolic elements. These interconnected symbols work together to reinforce Bastet's complex and multifaceted nature. The very form of the cat embodies her essence. Its swiftness and silent movements represent her ability to ward off unseen dangers. The cat's keen eyesight and sharp senses translate into Bastet's ever-watchful presence, safeguarding her devotees.

Adding to this symbolism is the frequent inclusion of a sun disc adorning Bastet's head. This celestial symbol underscores her connection to the divine realm, linking her power to the life-giving rays of the sun. Finally, palm trees, often depicted near Bastet, are potent symbols of fertility and life. Their presence reinforces Bastet's association with motherhood and the abundance she brings to her followers. Through these carefully chosen symbols, Egyptian artists ensured that Bastet's essence and the blessings she bestowed were forever ingrained in the hearts and minds of the people.

The Enduring Legacy of Feline Deities

The Egyptians' reverence for cats transcended mere symbolism and bloomed into a deeply ingrained cultural practice. Cats weren't just revered companions; they were seen as divine beings worthy of the highest honors. After death, felines were meticulously mummified, a practice typically reserved for pharaohs and revered individuals.

Elaborate cat cemeteries unearthed by archaeologists across Egypt stand as testaments to this extraordinary devotion. These elaborate burial sites contained not just mummified cats, but also offerings, funerary masks, and intricate sarcophagi – all meticulously crafted to honor these feline companions in the afterlife.

Although the worship of animal deities faded with the decline of Egyptian civilization, the Egyptians' deep respect for cats left an undeniable mark. This fondness for felines continues to resonate today, with cats remaining cherished companions in countless households around the world. Bastet's enduring legacy as both a fierce protector and a nurturing goddess perfectly encapsulates the powerful connection humans have forged with these enigmatic creatures. Cats possess a duality that mirrors Bastet's nature – fierce independence and a capacity for deep affection. This complex and captivating combination continues to draw us to them. The influence of feline deities stretches far beyond the sands of time. The captivating nature of cats has inspired countless artists and writers throughout history. We see this in the awe-inspiring statues of ancient Egypt depicting cat gods, and even in modern literature, with characters like Lewis Carroll's Cheshire Cat leaving an indelible mark on our imaginations. Even today, the watchful eyes and graceful movements of cats continue to hold a certain mystique, a subtle echo of the deep respect and veneration shown to them by the ancient Egyptians.

Chapter 2: Cats Across the Globe: Folklore and Mythology

The reverence for cats isn't confined to the sands of ancient Egypt. It bloomed far beyond that cradle of civilization, captivating cultures across the globe. These alluring felines have become deeply entwined with the very fabric of societies worldwide. Across continents and throughout history, cats have been draped in symbolic meaning.

From the revered περίπατοι (peripatoi) or "walkers of the night" of ancient Greece to the fierce Bastet of Egyptian mythology, these enigmatic creatures have embodied both the grace of the night and the power of a warrior. Prepare to be whisked away on a captivating journey This chapter unlocks the secrets of cat folklore and mythology! Revealing the diverse ways cultures have perceived and portrayed these fascinating felines.

Get ready to unearth a treasure trove of tales and beliefs where cats are celebrated as guardians, protectors, and harbingers of good fortune! Perhaps the most recognizable symbol of this positive association is the lucky Maneki-neko of Japan. This charming cat figurine, with its raised paw beckoning good fortune, has captured hearts around the world. Unlike some cultures that view cats as symbols of good luck, the Celts held a unique belief. They saw cats as guardians of the underworld, entrusted with guiding and protecting the souls of the dead on their journey to the afterlife.

Our exploration wouldn't be complete without venturing into the shadows. While some cultures revere cats, others have ascribed more ominous characteristics to these enigmatic creatures. A stark contrast to cultures that revere cats is found in medieval Europe. Here, black cats were viewed with suspicion and fear. They were seen as omens of bad luck and even associated with witchcraft, leading to their persecution. By examining cats through this diverse lens of folklore and mythology, we can begin to understand the rich and complex legacy they hold. From symbols of good fortune to harbingers of ill omen, we'll explore the full spectrum of positive and negative connotations these captivating creatures have held throughout history.

Lucky Felines: Harbingers of Fortune

Across the globe, cats are revered as lucky companions. This belief likely began with their practical skills as mousers. By keeping rodent populations down, cats protected valuable food stores and brought a sense of well-being to homes and communities. Over time, this appreciation for their practical role transformed into a belief in their mystical abilities to bring good fortune.

- **Japan:** The Maneki-neko, or beckoning cat statue, is a popular charm believed to attract wealth and good luck. The raised paw is said to beckon good fortune towards the owner, with the left paw beckoning customers and the right paw beckoning wealth.
- **Southeast Asia:** The Korat cat, a sleek shorthaired breed with heart-shaped eyes, is believed to bring prosperity to its owner. These cats are especially revered in Thailand, where they are sometimes called "Siamese lucky cats."
- **Western Cultures:** Black cats hold a place in folklore as harbingers of good luck, particularly in the British Isles and Ireland. This association likely stems from the black cat's connection with witches and the occult, which in some traditions were seen as wielders of powerful magic, including good fortune.

Feline Guardians: Protectors and Messengers

Cats haven't just earned a reputation as lucky companions; they've also been revered as protectors and spiritual guides throughout history. The Vikings, for example, deeply respected cats for their hunting skills and companionship. They believed these felines possessed a unique connection to the spirit world. Norse mythology even features Freya, a powerful goddess, riding a chariot drawn by two magnificent grey cats, symbolizing both fierce strength and profound wisdom.

Across the sea, the Scottish Highlands hold stories of the Sith Cat, a mythical feline creature said to possess the power of prophecy. This fairy cat was believed to guard homes from misfortune, a role likely inspired by the cat's keen senses and independent nature. In cultures where survival depended on vigilance and a connection to the unseen, these qualities instilled trust and admiration. The cat's ability to navigate the darkness silently and its seemingly otherworldly perception made it a natural symbol of protection and a bridge between the physical and spiritual realms.

The Shadow Side: Fear and Misconceptions

Despite their current status as internet celebrities and suppliers of endless amusement, cats haven't always enjoyed such a rosy reputation. In some cultures, fear and misconceptions have overshadowed their cuddly charm. Black cats, in particular, have been victims of persecution for centuries, especially in Europe and North America. During the Middle Ages, their association with darkness and the witch trials led to the demonization of black felines.

This negative perception likely stemmed from a confluence of factors. Their nocturnal habits made them seem mysterious and unpredictable, unlike the domesticated animals that shared people's daylight hours. Additionally, their independent nature led them to be seen with suspicion, especially when paired with solitary women who were often unfairly labeled as witches. Moreover, the Middle Ages was a time when the natural world was less understood. Cats' exceptional eyesight and hearing in the dark, along with their silent stalking abilities, fueled anxieties about their true nature. Since cats were most active at night, they were seen as creatures associated with the shadows and the potential dangers that lurked unseen. Even their hunting prowess, an instinct that made them valuable mousers, was often misconstrued as malice. These unfounded fears, born from superstition and a lack of knowledge, have had a lasting impact. Even centuries later, black cats still face prejudice in certain cultures.

Shifting Perceptions: A More Balanced View

Thankfully, attitudes towards cats are evolving. In many parts of the world, black cats are now considered symbols of good luck, especially in Britain and Ireland. A far cry from the Middle Ages in Europe, where black cats were vilified for centuries as companions of witches and symbols of bad luck, this shift in perception reflects a growing appreciation for these feline friends. This negative perception lingered for centuries, but thankfully, it's giving way to a more positive outlook. This shift can be attributed to several factors, including increased awareness about feline behavior and the growing popularity of cats as companion animals. Social media has also played a role, with countless videos and online communities celebrating the unique personalities and quirks of cats.

Even in regions where negative connotations about black cats persist, like parts of Eastern Europe and Asia, a shift is happening. People are starting to recognize the practical benefits of having a feline companion. Cats are natural-born predators, and their presence is an effective deterrent against rodent infestations. And let's not forget the undeniable charm of these creatures! Their playful personalities, independent spirits, and moments of cuddliness have won over hearts around the world. This growing appreciation, along with their practical contributions, is leading to a more nuanced understanding of cats and their place in our lives.

The Curious Case of the Cat: Contrasting Views Throughout History and Across Cultures

The contrasting views of cats throughout history and across cultures are a fascinating window into the complexities of human perception.

Here's a deeper dive into some potential explanations for these contrasting views:

- **Observation and Misinterpretation:** Early human interactions with cats likely involved observing their nocturnal habits, keen eyesight in the dark, and independent nature. These unfamiliar behaviors, coupled with a lack of scientific understanding, could have been misinterpreted. The silent stalking at night might have been seen as a connection with dark forces, while their aloofness could have been misconstrued as sinister cunning.
- **Religious Influence:** In some cultures, cats were revered as companions of deities or even worshipped as gods themselves. However, opposing religious factions might have demonized these beliefs, associating cats with the very things they opposed. This demonization could have led to negative connotations being attached to the cats themselves.
- **Cultural Fears:** The unknown often breeds fear, and cats, with their elusive nature and nocturnal activities, might have easily fallen prey to this. Darkness has long been associated with negativity and danger in many cultures. Since cats thrived in the dark, some cultures might have linked them to these negative forces, creating a perception of them as bad omens or harbingers of misfortune.

The kaleidoscope of myths and legends swirling around cats throughout history underscores the enduring mystery and fascination these creatures hold for humanity. For thousands of years, these creatures of veiled secrets have captivated us, transforming from revered guardians to symbols of prosperity. Their enigmatic nature continues to fuel our fascination. Understanding these contrasting views enriches our understanding of cats' cultural history and helps us form a more balanced perspective on their role in our world. We can move beyond simplistic ideas and appreciate the complex relationship between humans and these captivating creatures. By recognizing both the reverence and the fear historically associated with cats, we gain a more holistic perspective on these remarkable creatures, allowing us to appreciate them for their true essence.

Chapter 3: The Familiar Spirit: A History of Magical Partnerships

The cackle of a witch, the glow of a cauldron – these are just some of the images that conjure the archetype of the witch in our minds. But there's another figure often lurking in the shadows beside her: the familiar. This mysterious companion, often depicted as a black cat, embodies a powerful bond between the witch and the beast.

Chapter 3 plunges us into the rich history of familiars. We'll explore the very concept of a familiar, untangling its origins and the various forms it has taken across cultures. From helpful spirits to demonic helpers, familiars have played a multitude of roles in magical traditions. But why cats, you ask? This chapter delves into the enduring connection between these magical partnerships and their feline counterparts, examining how cats came to be so closely associated with witchcraft.

A Familiar by Your Side: Defining the Partnership

In the realm of witchcraft, a familiar is a supernatural entity believed to assist a witch in their magical practices. Traditionally, familiars could take many forms – animals, spirits, or even demons were said to serve as magical companions and aids.

The specific role of a familiar varied, but generally, they acted as:

- **Protectors:** Familiars were believed to safeguard the witch from harm, both physical and magical. Their presence might shield against negative energies or even warn of approaching danger.
- **Messengers:** These companions could be sent on errands, delivering messages to other witches or gathering information from the unseen realms.
- **Guides:** Familiars, through intuition or direct communication, could guide the witches in their magical pursuits, offering insights and aiding in divination.

The Rise of the Feline Familiar: A Historical Purr-spective

While various animals have served as familiars throughout history, cats hold a unique position in the lore of witchcraft.

The historical connection between witches and cats likely arose from a confluence of factors:

- **Independent Nature:** Cats are known for their independent spirit, a quality often associated with witches who defied societal norms. This shared trait might have fostered a sense of kinship.
- **Nocturnal Habits:** Witches were often seen as practitioners of nocturnal magic. Cats, with their keen eyesight and activity at night, became natural companions for these midnight musings.
- **Association with Intuition:** Cats are often credited with a heightened sense of awareness and intuition. Witches, who relied on intuition and inner knowing in their practice, might have felt a connection to these perceptive creatures.
- **Practical Benefits:** Beyond the magical, cats provided practical benefits. Their ability to control rodent populations protected valuable herbs and ingredients used in rituals.

Beyond Superstition: A Deeper Connection

The image of a witch stirring a bubbling cauldron, and a black cat perched ominously on her shoulder, is a scene burned into our collective consciousness. But the concept of the familiar, a magical companion assisting a witch, stretches far beyond this iconic feline stereotype.

Chapter 3 dives into the fascinating history of familiars. It's important to note that this concept isn't universally embraced within modern witchcraft practices. Some view the familiar as a concept more relevant to historical interpretations of witchcraft, shaped by folklore and the persecution of witches. However, some practitioners choose to focus on the positive aspects. They find a powerful connection by forming a bond with an animal companion, drawing meaning from the symbolism and deepening their connection with nature.

Whether embraced literally or interpreted symbolically, the enduring link between witches and cats remains a captivating crossroads. It weaves together threads of folklore, magical traditions, and humanity's insatiable curiosity about the hidden powers veiled within the animal kingdom. This chapter takes a deep dive into the history of the familiar. We'll explore how the concept has evolved across cultures and the many roles these magical companions have played. We'll also uncover the reasons why cats, specifically, became so strongly associated with witches.

Looking Ahead: A Journey of Feline Friendship and Magical Exploration

The following chapters unlock the secrets of the remarkable bond between humans and cats. Get ready to unlock the secrets to becoming BFFs with your cat! The key to unleashing the true power of cat magic lies in a relationship built on respect and understanding.

But before we begin trying out new spells and crafting rituals with our furry familiars, a deeper understanding of their behavior is fundamental. The following chapters will shed light on the fascinating world of cat communication and the subtle ways your feline friend interacts with the world. We've explored the rich history and captivating myths surrounding cats in magic. Now, it's time to delve deeper into the heart of this magical partnership – your feline companion!

This section of the book isn't just about understanding your cat; it's about unlocking a new way of communicating and collaborating. Learn to decipher the secret language of meows, body language, and tail flicks. Explore how different breeds might hold unique magical correspondences. Most importantly, discover how to build a strong, trusting bond – the foundation upon which any magical partnership thrives.

Get ready to transform everyday interactions with your cat into magical moments. As you gain a deeper understanding of your feline friend, you'll unlock hidden wisdom and a potent connection that enriches both your magical practice and your life. So, grab your favorite catnip toy, settle in with your purring companion, and prepare to embark on a journey of understanding, friendship, and feline-powered magic!

Chapter 4: Whiskered Wisdom: Decoding Feline Communication

By learning to "speak cat," you'll not only enrich your daily life but also unlock a deeper understanding of the subtle energies they bring to your magical practice. So, prepare to be surprised, delighted, and perhaps even a little bewildered as we dive into the enigmatic world of cats and discover the magic that awaits in this extraordinary partnership.

Part 2: Understanding Your Feline Companion

Your feline familiar may not utter incantations or brew potions, but they possess a rich language all their own. By learning to decipher their meows, body language, and subtle cues, you can unlock a deeper understanding of your cat and strengthen your magical partnership. This newfound communication will allow you to work together more effectively, unifying your intentions with your cat's natural magical abilities.

The Feline Lexicon: A Guide to Meows and Purrs

Cats are surprisingly vocal creatures, and their meows hold a variety of meanings. A short, single meow might signify a greeting, while a long, drawn-out meow could indicate hunger or a desire for attention. A trill, often accompanied by body language like raised tails and arched backs, can express excitement or even playfulness.

The purr, perhaps the most beloved feline sound, is often associated with contentment and affection. However, research suggests purrs can also have a healing quality. Consider a purring cat curled on your lap during a meditation session as a potential offering of healing energy, promoting relaxation and focus.

Body Language: A Visual Conversation

A cat's body language speaks volumes. Unlike the clear pronouncements of humans, their communication lies in a silent symphony of posture, gesture, and expression. Yet, for those who can learn to listen, this secret language unlocks a wealth of information about a cat's mood, intentions, and even their unique personality.

Here are some key postures and their potential interpretations:

- **Relaxed Posture:** A cat with a relaxed body, soft eyes, and a slightly curved tail generally feels content and secure. This is a prime opportunity for a calming magical ritual or a shared moment of meditation.
- **Arched Back and Fur Standing on End:** This posture indicates fear or aggression. Avoid magical workings that might further stress your cat.
- **Tail Held High with a Slight Curl:** This confident stance often signifies a playful mood – a perfect time to engage in some magical games or incorporate playful movements into your rituals.
- **Slow Blinking:** Often referred to as a "kitty kiss," slow blinking signifies trust and affection. This is a magical moment to connect with your cat on a deeper level, perhaps through a shared visualization or a loving intention sent their way.

The Eyes Have It:

Don't underestimate the power of a cat's gaze! Far from being aloof or mysterious, their eyes can be just as informative as their body language. From playful flickers to intense stares, each blink and pupil change offers a glimpse into your cat's emotional state and current focus.

Here's how to decipher their messages:

- **Direct Stare:** This can signal dominance or a challenge, especially if accompanied by a stiff posture or flattened ears.

- **Slow Blinks:** A slow, blinking gaze is a sign of trust and relaxation. It's like a feline wink, so respond with a slow blink of your own to show affection.
- **Intense Focus:** If your cat seems fixated on a particular spot, there might be unseen energy they're sensitive to. Consider if there are any drafts, electrical currents, or even potential pest activity that you might miss.
- **Wide Eyes:** Dilated pupils can indicate fear, excitement, or playfulness depending on the context. Paired with a crouched posture and flattened ears, it likely means fear. With a swishing tail and playful body language, it suggests excitement for play.
- **Narrowed Eyes:** Squinted eyes can indicate suspicion, aggression, or concentration. If your cat is staring with narrowed eyes and a tense body, it's best to give them space.
- **Rapid Blinking:** This can be a sign of irritation or anxiety. Pay attention to other body language cues to understand the source of their discomfort.
- **Following You With Their Gaze:** This can be a sign of affection, curiosity, or a request for something (food, attention, play).
- **Looking Away After Eye Contact:** If your cat makes eye contact and then quickly looks away, it might be a sign of shyness or appeasement.

Remember, cat communication is all about interpreting a combination of body language and gaze. By paying close attention to these subtle cues, you can gain a deeper understanding of your feline friend's thoughts and feelings.

Putting it All Together: A Magical Conversation

By combining these elements – vocalizations, body language, and gaze – you can begin on a fascinating journey of deciphering your cat's unique language. A low meow, punctuated by a flicking tail, might indicate frustration. Perhaps your feline familiar is politely suggesting you postpone the complex ritual you were planning and opt for a simpler practice tonight.

On the other hand, a rumbling purr and a gentle head nudge near your altar could be an invitation to incorporate them into your magical workings. Imagine the possibilities – working your intentions with the natural flow of your cat's energy, creating a magical synergy unlike any other.

Remember, communication is a two-way street. As you learn to interpret your cat's signals, respond with loving attention, respectful interactions, and magical practices that benefit both of you. Perhaps incorporate some calming herbs your cat enjoys into your incense blend, or create a special ritual space that caters to their comfort and curiosity.

The more you understand each other, the deeper the trust and respect that blossoms between you. This, in turn, strengthens the foundation of your magical partnership, allowing you to work together more effectively and unlock the true potential of your feline familiar's inherent magical abilities. With each meow, purr, and knowing glance, your bond grows stronger, paving the way for a truly remarkable magical collaboration.

Chapter 5: Breeds and Correspondences: Unveiling the Magic in Your Cat

Have you ever gazed into your cat's eyes and wondered what secrets lie within? Perhaps you've witnessed their uncanny ability to sense hidden emotions or their seemingly effortless grace that defies gravity. Every cat, regardless of breed, possesses a unique personality and a wellspring of magical potential waiting to be explored.

Chapter 5 dives into the fascinating world of cat breeds and their historical associations. By learning about these correspondences, we can gain valuable insights into the energies your feline companion might embody.

But remember, these are like stepping stones on a magical path, not rigid categories to confine your furry friend. Your cat's individual personality and the unique bond you share will ultimately determine their true magical essence. So, prepare to start on a journey of discovery, where every purr and playful pounce reveals a little more about the magic that resides within your feline familiar.

Siamese: Guardians of Communication

The Siamese cat, a creature of captivating beauty with its piercing blue eyes and distinctively vocal nature has held a place of mystique for centuries. In the ancient kingdom of Siam (modern-day Thailand), these regal felines were revered as temple cats, believed to possess a bridge between the physical and spiritual realms. Their keen intelligence and seemingly endless capacity for vocalization fueled the belief that they were guardians of communication, effortlessly moving between the spoken word and the whispers of the unseen.

The Siamese's association with communication finds a beautiful application in the realm of magic. The Siamese's keen awareness and vocal expressiveness make them prime candidates for mastering magic centered on communication. Perhaps their vocalizations hold the power to unlock forgotten languages, or even serve as a conduit for messages from beyond the veil.

Blessed with sharp minds and an unwavering gaze, Siamese cats hold the potential to excel in divination. Their ability to focus on the subtlest details allows them to interpret signs and symbols with an almost supernatural accuracy, unveiling hidden truths for those who can listen. The list of their magical talents might even encompass psychic awareness. The Siamese's ability to sense subtle shifts in energy could translate into a heightened perception of information beyond the physical world.

With these correspondences as your guide, a thrilling quest awaits! Prepare to unearth the extraordinary magical gifts that slumber within your Siamese companion. Experiment with incorporating your Siamese cat's vocalizations into your magical practice. This, along with creating a shared space for meditation and divination, could forge a stronger bond and unlock a whole new level of magical collaboration. Let this be the starting point for your magical exploration. The deeper you delve into the world of your Siamese, the more their true magical essence will unfold. Together, you'll build a partnership as rich and dynamic as their vocal expressions.

Maine Coon: Gentle Giants and Protectors

The majestic Maine Coon, with its flowing fur and imposing size, has long been revered as a gentle giant. These regal felines boast not only impressive physiques but also a temperament known for their sweetness and affection. Their inherent protectiveness translates beautifully into the realm of magic.

Historically, Maine Coons were prized mousers, their keen hunting instincts keeping homes clear of unwanted pests. This quality readily translates to the magical concept of shielding one's space from negativity or unwanted energies. Imagine your Maine Coon companion, a watchful guardian, acting as a barrier against negativity, ensuring a safe and harmonious environment for magical endeavors.

The Maine Coon's calm demeanor and peaceful presence make them ideal companions for meditative practices and rituals focused on inner peace and security. Their quiet confidence can be a source of grounding energy, helping you center yourself during magical workings. Picture yourself meditating alongside your Maine Coon, their rhythmic breathing mirroring your own as you delve into a state of tranquility.

Together, you create a sacred space of serenity, fostering a deeper connection to your inner magic and the magic that flows all around you. As you delve deeper into your magical practice with your Maine Coon by your side, their true potential as a protector and facilitator of peace will undoubtedly unfold.

The Enchantment of Fur Color

Fur color has held symbolic meaning throughout history, and these associations can extend to the magical realm.

Here are some potential correspondences:

- **Black Cats:** Often associated with mystery and protection, black cats can be powerful guardians in magical practices.
- **Orange Cats:** Their sunny disposition suggests an affinity for abundance, prosperity, and positive energy.
- **White Cats:** Symbolic of purity and new beginnings, white cats might be ideal companions for cleansing rituals or spells focused on fresh starts.
- **Calico/Tortoiseshell:** These tri-colored cats, often with bold personalities, could embody a vibrant mix of energies, making them versatile companions in a variety of magical practices.
- **Grey Cats:** Often associated with wisdom and balance, grey cats could be powerful allies in spells seeking neutrality, dispelling confusion, or finding inner peace. Their quiet observation skills might also lend themselves to divination practices.
- **Tabby Cats:** Tabby markings, with their intricate swirls and stripes, can symbolize journeys, transformation, and adaptability. These cats could be ideal companions for rituals involving change, growth, or navigating life's unexpected paths.
- **Ginger Cats (with white markings):** Ginger fur, often associated with sunshine and fire, combined with white markings symbolizing purity, could create a magical counterpart for healing rituals. Imagine the warmth of the ginger fur promoting vitality, while the white markings cleanse and purify the recipient of the healing magic.
- **Bicolored Cats:** Cats with a stark division of black and white fur represent duality and the balance between opposing forces. These companions could be powerful allies in spells seeking harmony, mediation, or understanding opposing viewpoints.
- **Smoked Cats:** The smoky appearance, with a subtle gradation of colors, could embody mystery, secrets, and the unseen world. These cats might be well-suited for shadow magic, divination practices that delve into hidden knowledge, or spells that connect with the spirit realm.

Beyond Breeds and Colors: A Unique Connection

Remember, these are just some starting points. The strongest magical connection comes from understanding your cat's individual personality and how it aligns with your own. Observe your cat's habits, preferences, and how they interact with the world around them.

Does your playful tabby radiate an energy perfect for incorporating into a joyous abundance spell? Perhaps your sleek Siamese seems drawn to the mysteries of the moon, inviting lunar-based rituals. Trust your intuition and allow your cat's unique essence to guide you in discovering the magic they bring to your practice.

The important thing is to celebrate the individuality of your feline familiar. They are not simply representatives of a breed or a color; they are magical beings in their own right, waiting to share their unique gifts with you on your magical journey.

Chapter 6: Building a Magical Bond: Trust and Respect

The foundation of any successful magical partnership with your feline familiar is trust and respect, a bond built on mutual understanding and affection. Cats, with their keen intuition and independent spirit, thrive in positive relationships. Before beginning fantastical magical adventures together, ensure your home is a haven of comfort and security for your cat. This means creating a safe space that caters to their natural instincts.

Carve out areas in your home with designated scratching posts and climbing structures to satisfy their need to sharpen claws and survey their domain from above. Offer a variety of cozy napping spots, from sun-drenched window sills to plush hideaways, where they can retreat for quiet contemplation or restful slumber. Establish a consistent routine for meals and playtime, providing them with a sense of predictability and stability. Most importantly, shower them with love and respect. A gentle head scratch, a playful swat at a dangling toy, or simply offering a calming presence – these seemingly mundane acts build a foundation of trust that allows your magical partnership to blossom.

Remember, a happy cat is a magical cat. When their physical and emotional needs are met, they'll be more receptive to exploring the wonders of magic alongside you. Their innate curiosity and playful energy can become powerful assets in your magical endeavors. As your bond deepens, a silent conversation unfolds, a communication that transcends words. You'll begin to understand their subtle cues, their flicking tails and rumbling purrs becoming whispers of guidance and support in your magical practice. With a foundation of trust and respect, your feline familiar won't just be a companion on your magical journey – they'll become an integral part of it, their unique magical essence weaving itself into the fabric of your practice, creating a partnership as remarkable as it is rewarding.

Building Trust Through Positive Reinforcement

Positive reinforcement training is a fantastic way to build a strong and trusting relationship with your feline familiar. Cats don't respond well to punishment or dominance-based training methods, unlike their canine counterparts. Positive reinforcement offers a far more rewarding path. By showering your cat with treats, and praise, and engaging in playtime for desired behaviors, you unlock a world of understanding and respect, laying the groundwork for a truly magical partnership.

Imagine this: Your cat calmly sits and waits patiently by the treat jar instead of leaping up and demanding attention. You reward this welcome behavior with a tasty morsel and a verbal "good kitty!" This positive interaction not only reinforces the desired behavior but also builds trust. Your cat learns that good things happen when they listen and follow your cues.

Positive reinforcement isn't just a training method; it's about building a positive emotional bond. Patience is essential. Think short, sweet, and successful! Training sessions should be brief bursts of focused activity, always concluding on a positive note to maintain your cat's interest. Incorporate activities they already enjoy, like a feathery lure or a laser chase, as rewards for desired behaviors.

This positive reinforcement helps establish a routine they'll look forward to, strengthening your bond. With each positive interaction, the dance of understanding begins. You'll learn to translate the symphony of your cat's meows and body language, while they become more receptive to your cues, creating a harmonious flow of communication.

Positive reinforcement sows the seeds of respect in your relationship with your cat. As these seeds take root, a foundation of mutual understanding flourishes. Positive reinforcement acts like sunshine, nurturing a garden of trust within your cat. As they learn to associate you with delicious treats, heartwarming praise, and playful sessions, a strong bond blossoms, fertile ground for a magical partnership to flourish.

Happiness and security unlock the true potential of your feline familiar. In this state, their playful energy and curiosity morph into potent magical assets, while their contented purrs might hold the key to a deeper form of magical collaboration, a secret ingredient waiting to be discovered. Embrace positive reinforcement, and watch as your relationship with your cat blossoms into one of trust and respect. This transformation won't just yield a well-behaved companion; it will unlock the door to a magical familiar of extraordinary potential.

Crafting a Feline Sanctuary: A Haven for Magic and Whiskers

Your home isn't just a dwelling; it's a kingdom to be explored by your feline companion. To unlock their full magical potential, create a haven that caters to their natural instincts and fosters a sense of security.

Here are some key elements to consider:

- **Vertical Territory:** Cats are natural climbers, drawn to high vantage points for surveying their domain. This isn't just a quirk; it's a vital instinct. Embrace their inner leopard by providing a variety of vertical spaces. Invest in sturdy scratching posts that double as climbing structures, allowing them to hone their claws and keep active. Consider installing cat trees with multiple platforms and levels, creating a personal jungle gym for exploration and relaxation. Strategically placed wall shelves can also provide a network of pathways and perches, allowing your cat to navigate your home with confidence and grace.

- **Stimulating Toys:** A bored cat is a mischievous cat. Keep their playful spirit ignited with a rotating selection of engaging toys. From feathery wands that mimic elusive prey to puzzle feeders that challenge their problem-solving skills, and cater to their natural hunting instincts. Consider toys with hidden compartments for treats, adding an element of surprise and reward to playtime. Rotate the toys regularly to maintain their novelty, ensuring your cat stays actively engaged and mentally stimulated.
- **Designated Resting Areas:** Every feline warrior needs a tranquil refuge. Create cozy hideaways where your cat can retreat for undisturbed naps or quiet contemplation. Cardboard boxes lined with soft blankets make excellent temporary havens, while commercially available cat caves offer a more permanent solution. Consider placing perches high up in secluded corners, allowing your cat to survey their surroundings while maintaining a sense of security. Remember, a well-rested cat is a happy cat, and a happy cat is a magical partner in crime – ready to embark on fantastical adventures with you.
- **Respectful Interactions:** Building a trusting bond with your cat is paramount in any magical partnership. Learn to read their body language. A twitching tail, flattened ears, or dilated pupils can signal stress or fear. If your cat seems overwhelmed, give them space to retreat to their safe haven. Let them initiate interaction on their terms – a slow blink, a gentle head nudge, or a soft purr are all signs of affection. Remember, your cat is an individual with their own preferences. Respecting their boundaries fosters trust and strengthens your connection, laying the groundwork for a magical partnership built on mutual understanding.

Sharing Your Magical Space

As you dive deeper into your magical practice, remember that your feline familiar's well-being is intricately woven into your success. A happy and content cat is a far more receptive partner in your magical endeavors. Remember, a happy cat is a magical cat! When you cater to their needs and well-being, the purrs of contentment they emit become a harmonious melody, fueling the atmosphere for magic to truly flourish.

Here are some ways to weave your cat's happiness into your practice:

- **The Allure of Calming Herbs:** Certain herbs, like catnip (always used responsibly and in moderation to ensure your cat's safety), possess calming and mood-lifting properties. Explore incorporating these into your rituals in ways that are safe and enjoyable for your cat. Perhaps a small pouch filled with dried catnip, tucked discreetly near your altar, can subtly enhance the atmosphere with its calming aroma.
- **A Sacred Space for Whiskers:** Create a designated space on your altar just for your cat. This could be a small, elevated platform or a cozy cushion where they can observe your rituals or even participate if they're comfortable. By offering them a dedicated spot within your sacred space, you acknowledge their role as a magical partner and validate their presence in your practice.

- **Respectful Participation:** Not all cats are comfortable being the center of attention during rituals. Some may choose to observe from a distance, while others might be drawn to investigate the sights and sounds. The key is to respect their boundaries. If your cat seems stressed or overwhelmed, allow them to retreat to their safe haven. However, if they show a genuine interest in participating, let them! Perhaps a gentle stroke of their fur during a grounding ritual or a shared moment of quiet contemplation can deepen your connection and weave a stronger magical bond.

Remember, a magical partnership thrives on trust and mutual respect. By incorporating elements that enhance your cat's well-being and allowing them to participate in ways that feel comfortable, you'll not only create a happier environment for your feline friend, but you'll also foster a magical partnership that is enriching and rewarding for both of you. Their contented purrs and playful energy can become powerful assets in your practice, and the love and respect you share will become a potent force fueling your magical endeavors.

A Journey of Mutual Respect

Building trust and respect with your feline familiar is a journey, not a destination. It takes time, dedication, and a genuine desire to understand their unique language of purrs, meows, and whisker twitches. By curating a positive and enriching environment, you lay the groundwork for a magical partnership unlike any other. This environment isn't just about scratching posts and cozy blankets; it's about creating a space where your cat feels safe, secure, and loved. It's about respecting their boundaries while offering them opportunities to engage with your magical practice on their own terms.

As your bond strengthens, a fascinating transformation unfolds. The playful swats that once seemed like random attacks become opportunities to practice agility spells. The rhythmic purrs that lull you to sleep morph into a form of positive energy, fueling your magical endeavors. Even the seemingly mundane moments of quiet companionship take on a deeper meaning. A shared gaze across the room becomes a silent conversation, a testament to the powerful connection you've cultivated.

The possibilities for magical exploration become limitless with a trusted feline companion by your side. Their natural curiosity can inspire new spells and rituals. Their keen senses can act as early warning systems, detecting subtle shifts in energy. Imagine incorporating their playful energy into a spell of lightheartedness, or their calming purrs into a healing ritual.

Remember, a magical partnership isn't about dominating your cat or forcing them to participate in your practice. It's about building a bridge of trust and respect, a connection that allows you to explore the wonders of magic together. As your bond deepens, you'll discover that the most potent spells and the most profound magical experiences often bloom from the seemingly ordinary moments of love and understanding shared between you and your feline familiar.

Part 3: Purrfecting Your Practice: Integrating Cat Magic into Your Practice

The stage is set! You've dove into the history of feline magic, learned to interpret your cat's subtle cues, and built a foundation of trust and respect. Now, the real adventure begins! It's time to integrate the wonders of Cat Magic into your practice and embark on a magical journey together.

Hold on to your whiskers! This section guides you through practical exercises and rituals designed to deepen your connection with your cat, sharpen your intuition, and awaken the unique magical potential they possess. Ethics and caution are key! This section unveils the secrets of incorporating cat-inspired elements like catnip or shed fur into your magical workings. Learn how to ethically and responsibly harness these potent ingredients, infusing your spells and potions with a touch of potent feline magic.

Prepare to begin a journey of self-discovery and feline-powered magic. Learn how to create rituals that resonate with both you and your cat, fostering a deeper connection and enriching your magical practice in ways you never imagined. So, grab your favorite crystals, gather some calming herbs (safe for cats, of course!), and get ready to weave the magic of your feline familiar into the fabric of your craft!

Chapter 7: Purrfecting Intuition: Exercises and Rituals for Connection

The connection you share with your cat isn't just about cuddles and playtime. It's a deeper link that reaches beyond the physical world, offering a glimpse into the realm of intuition and magic. Don't be fooled by the cuteness! Behind those captivating gazes lies a powerful sixth sense. Cats seem to possess an uncanny ability to sense unseen energies, their very presence acting like a bridge between our world and realms beyond. Their whiskers twitch, acting as divining rods, expertly navigating the unseen currents of energy that flow around us. These subtle vibrations, imperceptible to our human senses, hold no mystery for the feline kind. With their otherworldly awareness, are cats perhaps the whiskered gatekeepers, watchful observers at the doorway that separates our reality from the unseen? Their enigmatic gaze seems to pierce the veil, hinting at a deeper purpose.

This chapter dives straight into the heart of this extraordinary connection. Ready to take your magical partnership to the next level? This section offers a variety of exercises and rituals designed to strengthen the mystical bond you share with your feline familiar. The deeper the bond with your feline familiar, the more magical the synergy becomes. As you unlock their language of purrs and whisker twitches, you'll also experience a heightened sense of intuition, allowing you to navigate the unseen with newfound confidence. Prepare to become a cat whisperer! This section equips you to decipher the subtle language of your feline companion – the flick of a tail, the arch of a back, the hypnotic gaze. We'll then dive into the art of meditation and visualization, guiding you toward a state of heightened awareness where the veil between spoken words and pure understanding thins, allowing you to enter a realm of true interspecies communication with your cat.

The journey begins now. As you nurture the bond with your feline familiar, a hidden language unfolds. Their purrs become more than just a comforting sound; they transform into a bridge, leading you toward a deeper understanding of the unseen world. This connection unlocks not only their magical potential but also a wellspring of intuition hidden within you, waiting to be discovered.

Guided Meditation with Your Feline Familiar: Unlocking Intuition Together

Have you ever felt your cat's calming purrs quiet your mind and focus your energy? Meditation, a powerful tool for developing intuition, can be even more profound when shared with your feline companion.

Find a quiet space free from distractions and create a calming atmosphere. Here are some steps to guide you:

Finding Sanctuary (~5 minutes):

1. **Create a Calming Space:** Dim the lights and consider playing calming music like nature sounds or soft instrumental pieces (**optional**). Choose a comfortable position where your cat can easily join you, either nestled in your lap or curled up nearby.
2. **Ground Yourself:** Take slow, deep breaths, feeling your breath fill your lungs and belly with each inhale. As you exhale, release any tension and imagine roots growing down from your base, firmly anchoring you to the present moment.
3. **Mantras for Grounding:**
   "I am present."
   "I am calm and centered."
   "With each breath, I find peace."

Connecting with Your Cat (~3 minutes)

1. **Gentle Connection:** Gently close your eyes and focus on your cat. Notice their presence – the rhythmic rise and fall of their chest as they breathe, the soft

rumble of their purrs, the warmth of their fur against your skin (if they're on your lap).

2. **Shared Energy:** Visualize a cord of light, shimmering silver or gold, connecting your heart chakra (center of your chest) to your cat's heart chakra. Imagine this cord symbolizing the loving energy that flows between you.

3. **Mantras for Connection:**
   "We are connected, heart to heart."
   "Love flows between us, a bridge of light."
   "I am grateful for your presence."

Awakening Intuition (~3 minutes):

1. **Feline Light:** With your inner eye (your mind's eye), visualize a soft golden light emanating from your cat, filling the space around you. Allow this warm, luminescent light to bathe you, awakening your own intuitive senses. Imagine it gently activating your third eye chakra (located between your brows), enhancing your perception.

2. **Mantras for Intuition Activation:**
   "My intuition awakens, bathed in golden light."
   "I open myself to receive wisdom from within."
   "My senses are heightened, ready to perceive."

Shared Awareness (~5 minutes):

1. **Inner Landscape:** With your inner eye still open, imagine yourself exploring a peaceful landscape together with your cat. Is it a lush forest, a serene meadow, or a mystical mountaintop? Notice any sights, sounds, or feelings that arise. Pay attention to any messages or insights your cat might be trying to convey through subtle nudges, telepathic impressions, or vivid imagery.

2. **Mantras for Shared Awareness:**
   "We explore together, open to guidance."
   "I listen with my heart, open to receive."
   "Together, we navigate the inner landscape."

Gentle Return (~3 minutes):

1. **Returning to the Present:** When you feel ready, slowly bring your awareness back to the physical room. Wiggle your fingers and toes, gently stretching your body. Take a few deep breaths, feeling reconnected to your surroundings.

2. **Gratitude:** Open your eyes and express gratitude to your cat for their presence and participation in your meditation. Perhaps offer them a gentle head scratch or a soft word of appreciation.

This guided meditation is your springboard! As you practice regularly, personalize it to create a ritual that resonates with you and your feline friend. With each session, witness the blossoming of your bond and the awakening of your own intuitive senses. Remember, trust the process, be open to the subtle cues your cat offers, and embark on this exciting journey of self-discovery together.

Ritual of Shared Scrying: Unveiling the Unseen with Your Feline Familiar

The ancient art of scrying, where a reflective surface becomes a portal to hidden knowledge, takes on a whole new dimension with your cat by your side. Their presence can act as a catalyst, amplifying the insights gleaned from the swirling depths of the scrying surface.

Here's a simple ritual to invite your feline companion on a journey into the unseen:

Gathering Your Tools (Preparation - 5 minutes):

1. **Find a Quiet Sanctuary:** Locate a peaceful space free from distractions. Ideally, the room should be dimly lit, creating a more conducive atmosphere for scrying.
2. **Prepare the Scrying Surface:** Choose your reflective surface: a black mirror or a bowl filled with clean, black water. Both offer effective portals for scrying.
3. **Light the Candle of Clarity:** Place a white candle beside the scrying surface. The white flame symbolizes purity and illumination, guiding your journey into the unseen realms.
4. **Welcome Your Feline Familiar:** Ensure your cat feels comfortable and relaxed in the space. Perhaps offer them a familiar toy or scratching post nearby, allowing them to participate on their own terms.

Opening the Sacred Space (Optional - 3 minutes):

1. **Casting the Circle (For practitioners of circle magic):** If you practice circle magic, cast a circle to create a sacred space for your scrying ritual. Visualize a white light flowing from your hands, forming a protective barrier around the designated area.

Setting Your Intention (Centering - 2 minutes):

1. **Clearly State Your Purpose:** Before gazing into the reflective surface, take a moment to clearly state your intention for scrying. Are you seeking guidance on a specific issue, such as a decision or a challenge you're facing? Perhaps your intention is simply to deepen your connection with your cat on a mystical level.

Shared Focus and Observation (Scrying - 10-15 minutes):

1. **Gaze Together:** Gently gaze into the reflective surface, inviting your cat to observe alongside you. Maintain a relaxed focus, allowing your mind to become quiet and receptive.
2. **Notice the Subtleties:** Pay close attention to any images, symbols, or feelings that arise within your consciousness. Does your cat's presence influence the scrying in any way? Do their movements or vocalizations seem to hold any significance?

Interpretation and Integration (Reflection - 5 minutes):

1. **Record Your Insights:** After a set time (determined by your intuition), gently break focus and record any insights you received during the scrying session.
2. **Connecting the Dots:** Consider how your cat's behavior or presence might relate to the messages you received during the scrying. Did their actions or vocalizations seem to confirm or complement the symbols or images you witnessed?

Closing the Ritual (Optional - 2 minutes):

1. **Dissolving the Circle (For practitioners of circle magic):** If you cast a circle at the beginning, thank the directions (East, South, West, North) for their protection and dissolve the circle, visualizing the white light returning to you.
2. **Gratitude for Your Feline Companion:** Express gratitude to your cat for their participation in the scrying ritual. Perhaps offer them a gentle head scratch or a soft word of appreciation.

Remember: These are just starting points. As you explore the magic of shared scrying with your feline familiar, feel free to experiment with different exercises and rituals to find what works best for your unique bond. Trust your intuition, be open to unexpected messages from the unseen realms, and allow the extraordinary connection with your cat to guide your exploration of the magical world.

Chapter 8: Nine Lives of Spells: Working with Your Feline Familiar

The bond you share with your cat transcends the physical realm. Your connection with your cat is a symphony whispered in purrs, punctuated by the playful nips that speak volumes. It's a language that transcends words, a silent understanding that resonates on a soul-deep level. This chapter acts as your personal grimoire, a magical book filled with spells and rituals designed to ignite the extraordinary potential within your unique feline partnership. As you explore these practices, prepare to witness the blossoming of your connection and unlock a realm of magic where human and feline energies intertwine.

The magic you create with your cat isn't a one-size-fits-all recipe. It's a dance where trust, respect, and shared energy form the foundation. Remember, the most powerful spells come from personalizing these rituals to your cat's unique personality and comfort level.

Forget the stereotypical familiar as just a pet! Your cat possesses a playful spirit that can ignite your own creative spark, and their keen intuition can guide you towards surprising insights in the magical realm. Treat the spells and rituals here as stepping stones, encouraging you to cultivate and develop your own magical practice alongside your feline muse.

As you share experiences with your cat, the invisible thread connecting you grows stronger. This deepening connection acts as fuel, igniting the magical potential that lies within your unique partnership. Every play session, cuddle time, and shared adventure strengthens the magic you create together. Prepare to embark on a journey of self-discovery and wonder, where the purrs of your feline familiar become the soundtrack to your magical life.

Ethical Considerations: Working with a Willing Partner

The magic you create with your cat is a beautiful collaboration, but it's crucial to remember that this partnership thrives on respect and trust.

Here are some key ethical considerations to ensure your feline familiar remains a happy and willing participant:

- **Your Cat's Comfort Comes First:** Above all else, prioritize your cat's well-being. Never force them to participate in any ritual or activity that makes them feel stressed or uncomfortable. Cats are incredibly intuitive creatures, and their body language speaks volumes. Watch for signs of discomfort such as flattened ears, a swishing tail, or dilated pupils. If you observe any of these signals, immediately end the ritual and offer your cat a safe space to retreat.
- **Respect Their Boundaries:** Just like humans, cats have individual personalities and preferences. Some felines may be naturally curious and drawn to participate in magical practices, while others might prefer to observe from a distance. Respect your cat's boundaries. Don't pressure them to engage in activities that seem outside their comfort zone.
- **Create a Safe and Positive Environment:** Set the stage for a positive experience. Choose a quiet space free from distractions where your cat feels secure and relaxed. Offer them familiar comforts like a favorite blanket or scratching post. The goal is to create an atmosphere that fosters a sense of trust and allows your cat to participate on their own terms.
- **Focus on Shared Experiences:** The most potent magic often arises from shared experiences. Instead of forcing your cat into a specific role, focus on creating rituals that feel natural and enjoyable for both of you. Perhaps incorporate elements of play, like

chasing a toy infused with your intention, or create a calming meditation space where you can both relax and connect on a deeper level.

By prioritizing your cat's well-being, respecting their boundaries, and creating a positive environment, you ensure that your magical partnership remains a source of joy and connection for both of you.

Craft a Catnip Charm for Comfort and Protection

The gentle purr of a feline companion isn't the only benefit cats bring to our lives. They possess an inherent ability to sense and navigate energetic shifts, making them natural guardians. This charm pouch, infused with the comforting scent of catnip and the protective properties of amethyst (optional), offers a gentle shield for you or your home.

Gather Your Supplies:

- ☐ **A Small Pouch:** Choose a pouch that resonates with you. Fabric options like linen or cotton allow the catnip scent to permeate gently. Leather pouches offer a more durable option, but may require ventilation holes to prevent the catnip from losing its potency.
- ☐ **Dried Catnip:** Ensure the catnip is organic and safe for your feline friend to be around. Consider purchasing catnip specifically intended for crafting purposes, as it may be cleaner and more visually appealing than loose catnip.
- ☐ **Amethyst Crystal (Optional):** Amethyst is known for its protective and calming properties. A small, tumbled amethyst adds a touch of gemstone magic to your pouch, but it's not essential.
- ☐ **Cleansing Incense or Herb (Optional):** Garden sage, lavender, or cedar are popular choices for cleansing rituals. You can also use a cleansing spray formulated for crystals (if using amethyst).
- ☐ **Needle and Thread** (if using fabric) or **Leather Cord** (if using leather)

Preparing the Pouch:

1. **Cleanse the Pouch:** If you're using incense or a cleansing herb, light it in a safe and well-ventilated area. Waft the smoke over the pouch, visualizing any negativity or unwanted energy being carried away. Alternatively, you can use a cleansing spray appropriate for the pouch material (especially important for leather).
2. **Set Your Intention:** Hold the pouch in your hands and close your eyes. Focus on your desire for protection. Perhaps you envision yourself surrounded by a white light or imagine your home enveloped in a warm, secure energy.
3. **Charge the Amethyst (Optional):** If you're using an amethyst crystal, cleanse it alongside the pouch using the same method. Then, hold the amethyst in your hands and visualize it absorbing white light, becoming a beacon of protection.

Assembling the Charm Pouch:

1. **Fill the Pouch:** Place the dried catnip inside the pouch. If you're using an amethyst, add it now.
2. **Sew or Tie Shut (Fabric Pouch):** Using a needle and thread, carefully sew the pouch closed, securing the contents.
3. **Secure the Pouch (Leather Pouch):** If using a leather pouch, thread a leather cord through designated holes and tie it securely.

Using Your Protection Pouch:

- **Carry it with You:** Keep the pouch in your pocket or purse for personal protection throughout the day.
- **Place it in Your Home:** Choose a specific location within your home that feels intuitively right. Perhaps it's near the entryway, in your bedroom for a sense of security while you sleep, or in a central location to protect the entire space.

Remember, the catnip in this pouch will naturally lose its potency over time. When the scent starts to fade, consider replacing the catnip with fresh, organic catnip to maintain the protective properties of your charm.

A Purrfect Journey: Healing Visualization with Your Feline Companion:

Cats have long been revered for their calming presence and mysterious purring. Modern science is even catching up, with studies suggesting that a cat's purr can range from 25 to 150 Hertz, a frequency believed to promote bone healing, pain relief, and even tissue regeneration. This guided visualization harnesses the power of your cat's purr to guide you on a journey of self-healing and rejuvenation.

Preparation: Creating a Sanctuary for Healing (~5 minutes)

1. **Find Your Comfort Zone:** Locate a quiet space free from distractions. Settle onto a comfortable surface like a bed, couch, or yoga mat, ensuring there's enough room for your cat to join you comfortably. You can either have them curl up on your lap or nestle beside you.
2. **Dim the Lights:** Opt for soft lighting or candles to create a calming atmosphere. The gentle flicker of candlelight can be particularly soothing, but prioritize safety if you choose this option.
3. **Set the Mood with Calming Music (Optional):** Play calming music in the background, such as nature sounds, gentle classical melodies, or binaural beats specifically designed for relaxation. Choose music that resonates with you and creates a sense of peace.

The Purring Journey: A Guided Visualization (~10-15 minutes)

1. **Ground Yourself with Deep Breaths:** Begin by taking a few slow, deep breaths. Inhale deeply through your nose, feeling your belly expand. Hold your breath for a moment, then exhale slowly through your mouth, releasing any tension you might be carrying. Repeat this process for several breaths, allowing your body to relax and become present in the moment.
2. **Focus on the Purring:** Gently close your eyes and focus your attention on your cat's purr. Feel the rhythmic vibration travel through your body, starting from the point of contact (lap or nearby) and spreading outwards. Imagine the purr as a soothing wave, washing away any stress or discomfort you might be experiencing.
3. **Visualize the Healing Light:** As you continue to focus on the purring, imagine a soft, warm light emanating from your cat. See this light enveloping you completely, filling any areas of physical or emotional discomfort with a gentle, healing energy. Perhaps visualize the light mending specific areas of concern, or simply allow it to bathe you in its restorative glow.
4. **Basking in the Healing Energy:** Spend a few minutes basking in this warm, comforting light. Allow yourself to fully absorb the healing energy it provides, feeling any tension or discomfort melting away.

Grateful Closure (~2-3 minutes)

1. **Gently Return to Awareness:** When you feel ready, slowly bring your awareness back to the room. Wiggle your fingers and toes, gently stretching your body as you return to a state of wakefulness.
2. **Gratitude for Your Feline Companion:** Open your eyes and express your gratitude to your cat for their participation in your healing journey. Offer them a gentle head scratch, a soft word of appreciation, or a treat (if they're receptive).

Remember, this visualization is just a starting point. As you practice, feel free to personalize it based on your own needs and preferences. You can even incorporate affirmations or specific healing intentions into your visualization to further enhance the experience. With regular practice, you may discover the profound healing power that lies within the purr of your feline friend.

Unveiling the Unseen: Divination with Your Feline Familiar:

Cats, with eyes that seem to pierce the veil between worlds, have always been linked to intuition and the hidden realms. Their sharp senses and seemingly random behaviors can be a treasure trove of insights, waiting to be deciphered by those attuned to their subtle language. Prepare to be amazed! This chapter unveils the magic of feline-assisted divination. We'll explore how to interpret your cat's purrs, gazes, and even seemingly whimsical actions, transforming them into potent tools for deciphering hidden knowledge and embarking on a journey of self-discovery with your feline familiar by your side.

The Language of the Purr:

A cat's purr is more than just a sound of contentment. It's a symphony of subtle vibrations, each variation holding a potential message. By attuning yourself to the nuances of their purr, you can learn to decipher if your feline friend is relaxed and content, or perhaps picking up on unseen energy shifts in the environment. These subtle shifts in pitch, rhythm, and intensity can become a valuable tool for understanding your cat's emotional state and even gaining insights into the unseen world around you.

Here are some key interpretations to get you started:

- **The Steady Thrum:** A rhythmic, unbroken purr is often a sign of deep contentment and well-being. During meditation or rituals, this steady purr can indicate a harmonious flow of energy, a confirmation that you're on the right track.
- **The Broken Purr:** A purr that sputters or breaks occasionally might suggest your cat is picking up on unsettled energy or emotional dissonance. If this occurs during divination, take a moment to assess your own emotional state and consider if any unresolved issues might be clouding your focus.
- **The Crackling Purr:** A crackling purr, accompanied by a twitching tail, can sometimes indicate excitement or anticipation. In the context of divination, this might signify an upcoming event of significance, or a revelation waiting to be discovered.
- **The Silent Shift:** Pay close attention to any sudden changes in your cat's purring during your practice. A purr that abruptly stops might be a subtle nudge from your familiar, urging you to take a different approach or consider an alternative interpretation.

The Power of the Gaze:

A cat's gaze is a window into their soul. Those mesmerizing eyes, like pools of liquid gold or bottomless emerald, can communicate volumes without a word. A slow blink conveys trust and affection, while a dilated pupil might signal excitement or a heightened awareness of unseen energies. Learning to read the language of their gaze deepens your connection with your feline familiar and opens a doorway to a world of unspoken understanding.

Here's how to decipher some of the messages hidden within their eyes:

- **The Focused Stare:** If your cat seems fixated on a particular spot in the room, especially during divination practices, take note. Their gaze might be drawn to unseen energy or entities you haven't perceived. Trust their intuition and explore the object of their focus with an open mind.

- **The Slow Blink:** A slow, deliberate blink in your direction is a feline expression of trust and affection. During divination, this gesture can be interpreted as a sign of approval, indicating your familiar is comfortable with the direction of your practice and is offering their support.
- **The Dilated Pupils:** Wide, dilated pupils can indicate heightened awareness or excitement. If your cat's eyes widen during your divination session, it might signify they've picked up on a powerful energetic shift or a significant message waiting to be revealed.
- **A Journey of Co-Creation:** Remember, these interpretations are just a starting point. As you deepen your connection with your cat, you'll discover unique ways to incorporate their presence into your divination practice. Pay attention to their individual quirks and behaviors. Does your cat nuzzle a specific card during a tarot reading? Do they swat playfully at your pendulum, influencing its swing? These seemingly random actions might hold deeper meaning, revealing messages specific to your bond.

The key lies in approaching your practice with an open mind, a respectful heart, and a deep trust in your intuition. As you learn to interpret the subtle cues offered by your feline familiar, the magic you create together will blossom into a powerful tool for divination, self-discovery, and a deeper understanding of the unseen world.

Chapter 9: The Furry Ingredient: Ethical Use in Magic

Cats, those enigmatic creatures with a gaze that seems to pierce the veil between worlds, have captivated humans for millennia. Their independent spirit, keen senses, and uncanny intuition have long been associated with the magical realm. This chapter delves into the potential of incorporating cat-inspired ingredients into your magical practice while emphasizing ethical sourcing and respectful practices when working with your feline companion.

Throughout history, cats have been revered as guardians of the unseen realms, navigators of the astral plane, and even embodiments of luck and protection. Their very presence is imbued with a subtle magic, one that can be harnessed through the use of carefully chosen ingredients.

Consider incorporating the following into your spells and rituals:

- **Catnip:** This herb, beloved by felines for its euphoric properties, can be used to enhance spells of joy, playfulness, and connection. Think of it as a bridge, fostering a lighter energy and encouraging a playful spirit within your practice.
- **Cat Hair (Ethically Sourced):** A single strand of fur, shed naturally by your cat, can be a powerful way to personalize your magic. It acts as a physical link, embodying your feline

companion's unique energy and strengthening the bond between you. Remember, never pluck fur from your cat, and always prioritize their comfort by using only hair they've shed naturally.

- **Feathers (Ethically Sourced):** Feathers, particularly those from birds your cat might encounter in nature, can symbolize agility, grace, and the ability to navigate unseen realms. Incorporated into a charm or sachet, they can enhance spells focused on communication, swiftness, or connecting with the spirit world.

Respectful Practices: A Feline First Approach:

While the magical potential of cat-inspired ingredients is undeniable, it's crucial to prioritize ethical sourcing and respect for your feline companion. Here are some key guidelines:

- **Never Harm:** The well-being of your cat is paramount. Never use any ingredient that would cause them discomfort or distress. Focus on using naturally shed fur and ethically sourced materials.
- **Gain Their Consent (Symbolically):** While cats may not understand the intricacies of magic, consider offering them a treat or a playful session before incorporating any element of their essence into your practice. This symbolic offering strengthens the bond and ensures their participation is one of positive association.
- **Less is More:** A single strand of fur or a small, ethically sourced feather is all you need. Respect the power inherent in these feline-inspired ingredients, and use them sparingly for maximum effect.

By following these guidelines, you can create a magical practice that honors the spirit of your cat and unlocks the potential for a deeper, more meaningful connection. Remember, the magic you create together isn't just about the ingredients; it's about the love, respect, and shared journey you embark upon as magical companions.

A Legacy of Whiskered Magic

The bond between humans and cats transcends mere companionship. For centuries, these enigmatic creatures with eyes that pierce the veil have held a place of reverence within magical traditions. Their playful spirit, keen senses, and uncanny intuition have long been associated with the unseen realms, making them natural partners in the world of witchcraft and spellcraft.

Whispers from the Herb Garden: The Allure of Catnip

- Catnip is an herb that ignites feline euphoria with its potent aroma and has a rich history in magical practices. Its stimulating effect wasn't just observed in our furry companions; it was believed to enhance spells of joy, connection, and even divination. Cultures around the world saw catnip as a way to bridge the gap between the physical and the unseen, fostering a lighter energy and encouraging a playful spirit within rituals. Imagine catnip as a key that unlocks the doorway to your inner knowing, allowing you to tap into a sense of childlike wonder as you delve into the mysteries of the magical world.

A Feline's Touch: The Power of Shed Fur

- Shed fur, often seen as an unwanted byproduct of feline grooming, holds a deeper significance in the realm of magic. A single strand, naturally shed by your cat, can be a powerful way to personalize your magical workings. It acts as a physical link, imbued with your feline companion's unique energy. By incorporating this fur into spells or rituals, you strengthen the bond between you and your cat, creating a potent charm that resonates with their essence.
- Throughout history, various cultures have woven cat fur, particularly black fur, into protection charms. Some believed it warded off negativity or evil influences, while others saw it as a way to cloak yourself in the invisibility and grace of the feline form. However, a core value has always been paramount in these practices: ethical sourcing and respectful treatment of feline companions. A cat should never be harmed or distressed in the name of magic. Instead, focus on using naturally shed fur and ethically sourced materials, ensuring your feline friend remains a willing and cherished partner in your magical journey.
- The legacy of whiskered magic reminds us that the most potent tools often lie in the simplest elements. By incorporating catnip and shed fur into your practice, you not only honor the rich history of feline magic but also deepen your connection with your own furry familiar. Remember, the magic you create together isn't just about the ingredients; it's about the love, respect, and shared journey you embark upon as magical companions.

Ethical Sourcing: The Heart of Feline Magic

While these elements hold potential magical properties, ethical sourcing is paramount.

Here's how to ensure your feline familiar's gifts are used with respect:

- **Natural Shedding:** The most ethical approach is to collect fur your cat sheds naturally. Regularly brush your cat to gather loose fur, benefiting them while acquiring materials for your practice.
- **Respectful Collection:** Never pluck fur directly from your cat. This can be uncomfortable and stressful for them. Look for fur that accumulates on furniture, scratching posts, or your clothing.

- **Organic Catnip:** If using catnip in your rituals, ensure it's organically grown and safe for your cat to be around. Avoid commercially available catnip toys that might contain harmful additives.

Alternatives for the Discerning Witch

If your cat dislikes catnip, or you have ethical concerns about using fur, there are alternative ways to incorporate feline energy into your magic:

- **Symbolic Substitutions:** Use symbolic representations of catnip or fur. Black thread, a miniature cat figurine, or an image of a cat can hold the same intention in your rituals.
- **Herbal Correspondences:** Explore herbs associated with similar properties as catnip or fur. For instance, valerian root is known for its calming properties, mirroring the tranquility often associated with cats. Blackberry leaves might be substituted for black cat fur in protection spells due to their shared color.
- **The Power of Intention:** Ultimately, the most potent ingredient in your magic is your intention. A well-placed intention and a strong bond with your cat can make ethically sourced elements powerful. However, ethically sourced alternatives imbued with your focused will can be equally effective.

Magic thrives on respect and connection. By honoring your cat's well-being and using their essence thoughtfully, you create a magical partnership built on trust and mutual respect. Explore, experiment, and discover the unique ways to weave the magic of your feline familiar into the fabric of your craft.

Part 4: A Purrfect Partnership: Living a Magical Life with Your Cat

Ready to infuse your life with feline magic? This section goes beyond the typical spellbook, it empowers you to transform your everyday interactions with your cat into magical moments. Discover practical techniques that deepen your connection and enrich both your lives with a touch of the extraordinary. Unleash the magic that already exists in your shared bond!

Step into a world where your home becomes a testament to your cat's natural magic! Here, you'll discover ways to celebrate their spirit through your décor, create a shared meditation space infused with their calming presence, and even design rituals that elevate the simple joys of playtime and affection into magical experiences. Prepare to nurture a deeper connection with your cat by honoring their unique magic within your shared space.

Forget the grand gestures! The true magic lies in the everyday interactions you share with your feline companion. As you learn to appreciate their quiet wisdom and potent energy, your life will be infused with wonder, companionship, and the extraordinary magic that flows from your bond.

Chapter 10: A Sanctuary for Two: Where your Cat's Comfort Meets your Magical Practice

Your home is a haven, a sanctuary that nourishes your well-being and cultivates your magical practice. However, it's also the domain of another powerful spirit – your feline familiar. This chapter dives into the art of cultivating a magical space that celebrates the needs of both you and your cat.

Imagine your home as a shared sanctuary, where you can nurture your magical practice and your cat can feel comfortable and enriched. This chapter will guide you through creating a harmonious space that caters to both your needs. The goal is to create a harmonious environment where you can both thrive.

Here are some key considerations:

- **Feline Comfort First:** A happy cat is a key ingredient in any magical practice that involves your feline friend. Ensure their basic needs are met with comfortable perches strategically placed around your ritual space. Scratching posts and climbing structures not only provide enrichment but can also double as charging stations for their playful energy. Consider incorporating calming scents like lavender (safe for cats in small amounts) or catnip (used sparingly) to create a space they find inviting.
- **Boundaries and Respect:** Cats are creatures of habit, and respecting their boundaries is crucial. If your cat shows disinterest in your practice, don't force their participation. However, you can gently introduce them to the space with positive associations, offering treats or playtime beforehand.
- **Magical Touches with Catitude:** Subtly incorporate feline-inspired elements into your décor. Place statues of cats associated with good luck or protection, or hang tapestries with feline imagery. Scatter catnip-filled sachets around the perimeter of your sacred space (ensuring they're out of reach of curious paws). These subtle touches not only personalize your space but can also create a sense of inclusion for your cat, allowing them to feel like a valued participant in your magical journey.
- **Harmony Through Ritual:** Magical rituals can be opportunities to deepen the bond between you and your cat. Consider incorporating elements of play or affection into your practice. For example, if you're casting a spell for protection, you might include a playful swat at a toy imbued with protective sigils. Remember, the joy and connection you share with your cat are powerful forms of magic in themselves.

By creating a harmonious space that caters to both your needs and your cat's, you nurture a deeper connection with your feline familiar and transform your home into a sanctuary that vibrates with the magic of your shared journey.

The Purrfect Foundation: Understanding Your Cat's Instincts for a Magical Home

Food and toys are great, but a truly magical cat-friendly home goes deeper. This chapter emphasizes understanding your cat's inherent instincts and needs. By building this foundation, you can create a haven that empowers your magical practice and celebrates your feline companion's spirit. Don't be fooled by the purrs and playful swats! They are sentient beings with a complex range of behaviors and desires.

This chapter empowers you to connect with your cat on a deeper level, fostering a magical partnership that honors their unique essence. Take your magical practice to the next level! By attuning yourself to your cat's inherent nature, you become a whisperer of feline needs. This newfound understanding empowers you to create a magical space that fosters your own practice while celebrating and supporting the well-being of your furry companion.

Decoding the Feline Code:

Cats, with their independent spirit and keen senses, have evolved with a unique set of instincts.

Here are some key aspects to consider:

- **The Hunters' Den:** Cats are natural predators, with an ingrained need for stalking, climbing, and pouncing. Creating a vertical environment with strategically placed shelves, scratching posts, and cat trees provides outlets for these instincts and helps them feel secure within their domain.
- **Cleanliness is Key:** Cats are fastidious creatures, and a clean litter box is paramount to their well-being. Consider multiple litter boxes placed in quiet, easily accessible locations. Regular scooping and cleaning are essential to keep your cat comfortable and deter them from eliminating outside the designated area.
- **A Place to Call Their Own:** Cats crave security and a sense of ownership. Provide designated spaces for them to retreat and relax, such as cozy cat beds placed in quiet corners or high perches that offer a sense of control over their environment.

Understanding these fundamental needs not only ensures your cat's happiness and comfort but also lays the groundwork for a magical co-existence. A happy, well-adjusted cat is more likely to be receptive to your magical practice, creating a harmonious foundation for a shared sanctuary that vibrates with the magic of your unique bond.

Here's how to create a harmonious environment:

- **Vertical Territory:** Cats love to climb and perch. Offer scratching posts, cat trees, or shelves positioned at different heights. These vertical elements can also double as magical sigils, incorporating them into your space with intention.
- **Stimulating Sanctuary:** Provide a variety of toys to keep your cat entertained. Rotate them regularly to maintain interest, and choose toys that encourage their natural hunting instincts. Consider incorporating these toys into playful rituals that celebrate your cat's energy.
- **Calming Scents:** Certain herbs can enhance the magical atmosphere of your home while also providing a calming influence for your cat. Catmint, for instance, has a milder effect than catnip but offers a pleasant scent. Valerian root, known for its relaxing properties, can be placed in sachets around your home (out of your cat's reach) to create a tranquil environment.

Weaving Magic into the Everyday

Your cat's presence is inherently magical. Here are some ways to celebrate that magic in your everyday life:

- **Crystals for Harmony:** Place crystals associated with protection and intuition, like amethyst or black tourmaline, around your home. These crystals can create a sense of security for both you and your cat.
- **Sacred Space for Shared Moments:** Designate a specific area in your home for meditation or rituals. This space can be as simple as a corner with a comfortable cushion for you and a designated resting spot for your cat. As you practice your magic, invite your cat to join you if they're comfortable. Their presence can deepen your connection and enrich your practice.
- **Playtime as Ritual:** Play sessions with your cat can be transformed into playful rituals. Imbue your cat toys with positive intentions of joy, vitality, or agility. As you engage in playtime, visualize these energies flowing between you and your feline companion.

Your cat is a sentient being, not a decorative element. Allow them to choose their level of participation in your rituals. A safe, comfortable space filled with love and respect will naturally encourage them to be present and share in the magic you create together.

By creating a magical home that caters to both your needs, you nurture a deeper bond with your feline familiar and transform your everyday life into a beautiful expression of shared magic.

Chapter 11: Nine Lives, Ninefold Magic: Honoring Your Feline Familiar's Legacy

Cats haven't just been companions; they've become cultural icons. For millennia, whispers of their magic have echoed through folklore and mythology, their enigmatic presence woven into the fabric of human imagination. These mesmerizing creatures, with eyes that pierce the veil, continue to spark a sense of wonder, leaving an indelible mark on cultures across the ages. Legends throughout history have associated them with the mystical number nine – nine lives symbolizing not just longevity, but also rebirth, transformation, and the cyclical nature of existence. This concept resonates deeply in the realm of magic, where cycles of growth, release, and renewal are paramount.

This chapter dives into ways to celebrate these qualities of your feline familiar through magical rituals and practices. By honoring the unique bond you share, you not only deepen your connection with your cat but also tap into a potent wellspring of magical energy.

Unveiling the Ninefold Enchantment:

- **Rituals of Renewal:** Cats, with their ability to seemingly vanish and reappear, have long been associated with rebirth and renewal. Designate a specific ritual to celebrate these qualities, perhaps during the new moon – a time of fresh beginnings. You could incorporate symbolic elements like catnip (representing new growth) or a cleansing smoke cleanse with herbs like lavender (associated with purification) to refresh the energy within your home.
- **Embracing the Cycles:** The concept of nine lives also speaks to the cyclical nature of life, death, and rebirth. Consider incorporating this concept into rituals focused on healing or letting go. For instance, during a waning moon (a time of release), you could create a charm pouch filled with shed fur (representing past experiences) and moonstone (associated with intuition) to symbolize the release of negativity and the opening to new possibilities.
- **Honoring the Feline Spirit:** Cats are often seen as guardians of the unseen realms, navigating the astral plane with ease. Celebrate this aspect of their nature through meditations or visualizations where you invite their watchful presence to guide you. Focus on the feeling of security and protection their presence brings, allowing their energy to bolster your own during magical workings.

By incorporating these ideas and exploring your own creative interpretations, you can create a magical practice that honors the legacy of your feline familiar. Remember, the most potent magic often lies in the simplest gestures of love, respect, and appreciation. As you celebrate the ninefold enchantment of your cat, you not only deepen your bond but also unlock a unique wellspring of magic that flows from your shared journey.

Seasonal Celebrations with Your Feline Familiar

The changing seasons offer natural opportunities to connect with your cat's magic. As the days lengthen and nature awakens in spring, celebrate new beginnings and playful energy with your feline friend. Conversely, the quieter, introspective days of winter invite rituals of protection, meditation and shared warmth, creating a deeper sense of connection with your furry familiar.

Here are some ideas for incorporating them into your practice:

- **Spring Equinox - Renewal and Vitality:** Celebrate the spring equinox with a ritual focused on new beginnings and vitality. Sprinkle catnip (ensuring it's safe for your cat to be around) around your home to invite fresh energy. Engage in a playful session with your cat, visualizing them brimming with health and zest for life.
- **Summer Solstice - Confidence and Playfulness:** The summer solstice is a time to honor the sun's radiant energy. Place a sunstone (kept out of your cat's reach) on your altar, symbolizing confidence and vitality. Incorporate your cat's favorite toys into a playful ritual, celebrating their natural hunting instincts and joyful spirit.
- **Autumn Equinox - Gratitude and Inner Peace:** As the leaves change and the days grow shorter, the autumn equinox invites reflection and gratitude. Light a white candle and place dried chamomile (safe for cats) beside it, fostering feelings of peace and contentment. Spend quiet time curled up with your cat, expressing gratitude for their presence in your life.
- **Winter Solstice - Protection and Intuition:** The winter solstice marks the longest night of the year, a time for introspection and protection. Place black tourmaline crystals (out of your cat's reach) around your home to create a sense of security. Practice a guided meditation with your cat, focusing on inner guidance and intuition.

Life Cycles and Transitions: Rituals of Passage with Your Feline Familiar

Cats, with their profound connection to the unseen realms and their uncanny ability to navigate transitions, can offer invaluable support during life's turning points. Their presence can act as a calming anchor during times of uncertainty, and their keen intuition can guide us towards new beginnings and positive change. By incorporating them into our rituals, we not only honor the deep bond we share but also tap into a potent wellspring of magical energy that flows from their unique perspective.

Here are some ways to incorporate them into your rituals, honoring the profound bond you share and inviting their unique energy to guide you through these significant moments:

Welcoming a New Feline Familiar:

The arrival of a new furry friend is a cause for celebration! Create a welcoming ritual that sets the stage for a harmonious relationship. This simple act of acknowledgment honors the new chapter you're embarking on together, cultivating trust and a sense of belonging for your feline companion as they adjust to their forever home.

Here are some ideas:

- **Cleansing the Space:** Burn a cleansing herb like rosemary (safe for cats in small amounts and well-ventilated areas) to clear any stagnant energy and create a fresh, welcoming atmosphere. Open windows to allow the smoke to carry away any negativity.
- **A Bowl of Tranquility:** Place a shallow bowl of water infused with amethyst crystals (outside their reach) near their designated resting area. Amethyst is associated with calming energy and can promote a sense of security and peace for your new feline companion as they adjusts to their new home.
- **Scent of Welcome:** Sprinkle a small amount of calming catnip (use sparingly) on scratching posts or toys to create positive associations with their new environment. Catnip, known for its stimulating effect on felines, can help alleviate any initial stress or anxiety they might be experiencing.

Honoring the Loss of a Feline Companion:

The loss of a beloved cat can be a deeply painful experience. Creating a commemorative space allows you to celebrate their memory and find solace in the love you shared. This act of remembrance not only honors the unique bond you had with your feline companion but also provides a space for healing and processing your grief.

This space can serve as a sanctuary for your grief, a place to revisit cherished memories and feel the warmth of their presence even in their absence. Consider incorporating calming elements like flickering candles or soothing music to create a peaceful atmosphere for reflection and gentle goodbyes. As you reflect on the memories you cherish, their presence will continue to resonate within your heart, forever a part of your magical journey.

Here are some ways to create a sacred space for reflection:

- **A Sanctuary of Memories:** Establish a dedicated area for remembering your feline companion. Display cherished photos, their favorite toy, or a cozy bed they loved to curl up in.
- **The Light of Remembrance:** Light a white candle, symbolizing purity and peace, and spend time reflecting on the memories you shared. Recall their playful antics, their comforting purrs, and the unique bond you built together. Sharing stories and memories with loved ones can also be a helpful part of the healing process.
- **Whispers on the Wind:** Consider writing a heartfelt letter to your cat expressing your love and gratitude. Read it aloud, or burn it safely outdoors (ensuring no ashes remain near open flames), releasing your message on the wind as a symbolic act of letting go.

Think of these suggestions as stepping stones on your magical path. Feel empowered to adapt them or create entirely new rituals that resonate with the essence of your connection with your cat. The most important aspect is to find ways to express your love and appreciation, honoring the profound paw print your feline friend left on your soul.

Embrace the magic that blossoms as you celebrate the cycles of nature alongside your beloved cat. Each shared experience becomes a thread woven into a tapestry that honors the legendary nine lives and the enduring connection you share. Let your love and appreciation be the guiding light as you embark on this magical journey together.

Chapter 12: Astral Travel with Your Feline Familiar: Journeying Beyond the Veil

Throughout history, these captivating creatures have been revered as more than just companions; they've been seen as spirit guides and guardians, with a unique ability to navigate the unseen planes of existence. Whispers of feline magic echo through folklore and mythology, depicting them as familiars, watchful protectors who bridge the veil between our world and the next.

This chapter looks into a possibility that has ignited the imaginations of cat lovers for centuries: astral travel with your feline familiar. Astral travel, the act of projecting your consciousness beyond the physical body, can be a deeply personal and transformative experience. But what if you weren't alone on this journey? Could the profound bond you share with your cat extend beyond the physical, allowing you to explore the unseen realms together?

This possibility is intriguing, not just for the potential adventures it opens up, but also for the deepened connection it can create with your feline friend. Imagine journeying through astral landscapes, guided by your cat's intuitive understanding of the unseen. Perhaps they would act as your navigator, their inherent connection to these planes paving the way for a shared exploration filled with wonder and discovery.

Astral travel with your cat is a powerful tool for deepening your connection and unraveling the mysteries of their enigmatic nature. Imagine journeying together, your cat acting as a guide through the unseen realms. This exploration fosters a deeper understanding and appreciation for your feline companion, creating a bond that transcends the physical world. This chapter will equip you with the knowledge and practices to begin exploring this exciting possibility, offering guidance on preparing yourself and your feline companion for a magical journey beyond the veil.

Astral Travel: A Journey Beyond the Body

Astral travel, also known as astral projection, is the practice of consciously projecting your consciousness outside your physical body. While experiences vary, many describe astral travel as a vivid journey through unseen realms, filled with potential for self-discovery and exploration. Some believe this journey can be undertaken with a trusted companion, and for many cat owners, that companion is their beloved feline friend.

The Feline Guide: A Purrfect Companion

Cats, with their keen intuition and connection to the unseen, are believed to be natural astral travelers. Their presence can offer valuable guidance and protection during your astral journeys. Imagine your cat acting as a trusted navigator, their inherent understanding of these planes paving the way for a safe and awe-inspiring exploration together.

Benefits of Astral Travel with Your Cat:

- **Enhanced Awareness:** Cats possess a heightened awareness of subtle energies and unseen realms. Their senses are far more attuned than ours, allowing them to perceive vibrations and entities beyond our physical limitations. During astral travel, their presence can act as an anchor, grounding you and guiding you through unfamiliar astral landscapes. Imagine your cat acting like a beacon, their natural ability to navigate these planes helping you traverse uncharted territory with a sense of security.
- **Increased Confidence:** Having your feline companion by your side can bolster your confidence during astral travel, especially if you're new to the practice. Their calming presence can ease any anxieties you might have about venturing beyond the physical body. Additionally, their natural curiosity and adventurous spirit can be contagious, encouraging you to explore the astral realms with a sense of openness and wonder.
- **Deeper Connection:** Sharing an astral experience with your cat can be a profoundly transformative experience, deepening your bond in ways you never imagined. As you journey together through these unseen realms, you might gain unique insights into their

inner world – their perceptions, emotions, and perhaps even past experiences. This shared exploration fosters a deeper level of communication and understanding, solidifying the unique connection you share with your feline familiar.

Risks and Safety Precautions:

As with any exploration beyond the physical realm, there are potential risks associated with astral travel. It's important to approach this practice with respect and caution. Some believe that venturing into the astral plane can leave your physical body vulnerable, or that you might encounter disorienting or even negative entities.

Additionally, the experience of separating from your physical body can be unsettling, especially for beginners. This chapter will not only guide you through preparing yourself and your cat for astral travel but will also equip you with techniques for protection and safe astral navigation.

Here are some safety precautions to keep in mind:

- **Preparation is Key:** Ensure you're well-rested and in a relaxed state before attempting astral travel. Grounding exercises, such as spending time in nature or focusing on your breath, can help you prepare mentally and energetically. Additionally, create a dedicated astral travel space free from distractions. Dim the lights, use calming music, and ensure a comfortable position for your physical body.
- **Set Clear Intentions:** Before embarking on your astral journey, set clear intentions for what you hope to achieve. This will help guide your experience. Do you wish to explore a specific location, connect with a spirit guide, or simply deepen your bond with your cat? Focus on these intentions during meditation and visualize yourself successfully completing your astral journey.
- **Respect the Boundaries:** The astral realm can be vast and overwhelming. Don't stray too far from your familiar or attempt to explore areas that feel unsafe. Trust your intuition and pre-establish a "safe word" or visualization technique to signal your desire to return to your body. Experts recommend remaining close to your physical body during initial attempts, gradually venturing further as you gain experience.
- **Communication is Key:** Develop a method of communication with your cat in the astral realm. This could be through telepathic thoughts, shared feelings, or visual cues. Practice beforehand in your waking state, establishing a simple system for basic communication like "yes," "no," or indicating danger. The stronger your real-world bond with your cat, the more likely you are to achieve effective communication during your astral travels.

Preparing for Your Feline-Guided Astral Journey:

Strengthen Your Bond:

The foundation of safe and successful astral travel with your cat lies in a strong bond. When your cat trusts and feels comfortable with you, they'll be more likely to participate willingly and feel secure during the astral journey, creating a more positive experience for both of you. Consider this astral travel an extension of your earthly connection, deepening your understanding and communication with your feline companion on a whole new level.

Here's how to cultivate that connection:

- **Create a calm and loving environment:** Cats are sensitive to energy. Make sure your space feels peaceful and positive. Spend quality time cuddling, playing, and simply being present with your cat.
- **Practice relaxation techniques together:** Try guided meditations or visualization exercises specifically designed for pet relaxation. You can find many resources online or in pet wellness books.
- **Develop a communication system:** Pay attention to your cat's subtle cues like body language, purrs, and meows. Learn to interpret them as potential signs of their willingness or resistance to astral travel.

Create a Safe Space:

Prepare your astral travel space to optimize the experience for both you and your cat. Create a calm and inviting atmosphere with soft lighting and familiar scents, like your cat's favorite blanket or calming essential oils (safe for cats, of course!). This will ensure your feline friend feels secure while you embark on your astral journey.

- **Dim the lights and eliminate distractions:** A quiet and dimly lit space helps your body and mind relax and enter a receptive state. Turn off electronics and create a serene atmosphere.
- **Prepare a cozy spot for your cat:** Provide a familiar and comfortable bed or blanket specifically for your cat during the astral travel attempt. Place it near you so they feel secure and connected.
- **Consider using crystals or calming scents:** Some believe crystals like amethyst or selenite can promote astral travel. You can also use calming essential oils like lavender (diluted and used safely around pets!) to create a peaceful atmosphere.

Intention Setting:

Before entering the astral realm, set clear intentions for your journey with your cat: Visualize what you want to experience together, whether it's exploring a familiar location or venturing into a completely new world. This focus will guide your astral travel and strengthen the connection between you and your feline companion. Imagine your cat leading the way, their natural curiosity guiding you both on an unforgettable adventure.

- **Define your goals:** Do you seek specific information from the astral plane? Are you hoping to connect with a deceased pet? Having a clear purpose can guide your experience.
- **Communicate with your cat (telepathically):** While silent communication may be the goal, you can try gently expressing your intentions to your cat beforehand. This may help them feel more involved and trusting of the process.
- **Visualize your journey together:** Before attempting astral travel, spend some quiet time visualizing yourself and your cat exploring a chosen destination on the astral plane. This can help focus your intention and create a shared experience.

The Journey Begins:

- Relax your body and focus on your breath. Visualize yourself separating from your physical body, rising upwards. Reach out with your mind to your cat, inviting them to join you. If they're receptive, you might feel a sense of connection or see them appear beside you in their astral form.
- Together, explore the astral realm. Pay attention to your senses, feelings, and any insights that arise. Communicate with your cat through telepathic thoughts or shared visuals.

Returning and Grounding:

- When you feel it's time to return, gently draw yourself back to your body. Visualize re-entering your physical form. Wiggle your fingers and toes, feeling your connection to the earth. Take a few deep breaths to ground yourself fully.

Processing the Experience:

- After your journey, take time to journal your experiences. Write down any insights, messages, or symbols you encountered. Discuss your experience with your cat through gentle petting and positive reinforcement, letting them know you appreciate their presence.

Remember, astral travel with your cat is a potent and personal experience. Respect the process, prioritize your safety, and allow the journey to unfold organically. With a strong bond, clear intentions, and a sense of respect for the unseen world, your feline familiar can be a powerful guide on your astral adventures.

Chapter 13: Catnip and Other Herbs for Feline Magic

Cats and herbs have a long and fascinating history, intertwined in both the natural world and the realm of magic. This chapter explores the magical properties of certain herbs, their uses in feline-focused magic, and how to incorporate them safely and ethically into your practice while keeping your feline companion's well-being at the forefront.

The Allure of Catnip:

The most well-known herb in the feline world is undoubtedly catnip (Nepeta cataria). Its euphoric effect on many cats is legendary, sending them into rolling, head-bobbing bliss – a state some believe enhances their receptivity to subtle energies.

Magically, catnip can be used to:

- **Attract positive energy:** Sprinkle dried catnip around your ritual space to create a light and playful atmosphere. Focus on the areas where you'll be moving or interacting the most. Be mindful of the amount, however, as too much can be overstimulating for both you and your cat. **Start with a small pinch** and observe the energy in the space. **You can always add more later if needed.**
- **Enhance communication:** Catnip is associated with heightened senses and intuition. Burning catnip incense (away from your cat, with proper ventilation) or placing a small pouch of dried leaves near your meditation area may aid in deeper focus and receptivity during spells or divination. Consider incorporating other herbs that complement catnip's properties, such as chamomile for enhanced relaxation or rosemary for sharper focus.

Beyond the Catnip Patch:

While catnip holds a unique place in feline magic, other herbs offer valuable tools for the practitioner:

- **Valerian Root (Valeriana officinalis):** This herb, known for its calming properties, can be used to create a tranquil space for both you and your cat during rituals. Place a small amount of dried valerian root in a sachet and tuck it beneath a meditation cushion or place it near your cat's favorite resting spot. Remember, valerian root can be potent. **Start with a small amount and monitor your cat's reaction.**
- **Lavender (Lavandula angustifolia):** This versatile herb is known for its relaxing and stress-reducing properties. A few drops of diluted lavender essential oil diffused in the air (away from your cat) can create a calming atmosphere for both you and your familiar. Alternatively, you can stuff a small fabric pouch with dried lavender and place it near your designated ritual space.

Ethical and Safe Herb Use:

When using herbs in your practice, it's crucial to prioritize your cat's safety and well-being. Their curiosity can sometimes lead them to ingest things they shouldn't. Research each herb thoroughly before introducing it into your home, and remember, a cat's sense of smell is far stronger than ours. Opt for milder forms like dried leaves or sachets over essential oils, which can be overwhelming or even toxic to them. And remember, a cat's happy purr is always the most potent magical ingredient.

Here are some key points to remember:

- **Always use organic, pet-safe herbs:** Avoid any herbs treated with pesticides or chemicals. Cats are incredibly sensitive to toxins, so opt for organic varieties specifically labeled as pet-safe. These will be free of harmful residues that could make your feline friend sick.
- **Less is more:** Start with a very small amount and observe your cat's reaction. A little goes a long way, especially with catnip and valerian root. Monitor your cat for any signs of overstimulation, such as excessive rolling, dilated pupils, or aggression. If this occurs, remove the herb immediately.
- **Never force herbs on your cat:** If they show any disinterest or discomfort, discontinue use. Remember, your cat is an individual with their own preferences. If they seem disinterested in a particular herb, don't pressure them. There are plenty of other feline-friendly options to explore. Discontinue use immediately if your cat exhibits any signs of discomfort, such as sneezing, watery eyes, or difficulty breathing.

- **Be mindful of essential oils:** Many essential oils are toxic to cats. Their sensitive respiratory systems can be easily irritated by these concentrated fragrances. Diffuse essential oils in a well-ventilated room with your cat absent, ensuring the area is completely clear before allowing them back in. Never apply essential oils directly to your cat or their bedding.

Herb Magic in Harmony with Your Cat:

Infuse your magical practice with the subtle power of herbs, creating a space that benefits both you and your feline companion.

Here are some ways to approach this herbal magic, keeping your cat's well-being at the forefront:

- **Respect their Boundaries: Option 1:** Let your cat be your guide. If they're drawn to a particular herb, explore its magical properties and incorporate it subtly into your practice. **Option 2:** If your cat isn't interested in herbs directly, focus on creating a calming, welcoming atmosphere. Their presence itself can be a powerful magical conduit.
- **Embrace the Natural:** Surround your ritual space with plants known for their positive energy, like spider plants or ferns (ensure the plants are cat-friendly). These provide a natural, feline-friendly alternative to loose herbs.
- **Scentsational Spells:** Instead of using essential oils, create enchanting herbal sachets filled with dried catnip, lavender, or other safe herbs. Tuck these sachets near your meditation area or place them strategically around your home to create pockets of positive energy.

Alternatively:

- **Let Your Cat Lead the Way:** Observe your cat's interaction with certain herbs. Perhaps they're drawn to the playful energy of catnip or the calming scent of chamomile. Allow their natural inclinations to guide your herbal selections.
- **Create a Shared Herbal Sanctuary:** Designate a specific area for your cat that incorporates their favorite herbs, whether it's a cozy bed stuffed with dried lavender or a scratching post sprinkled with catnip (used sparingly). This shared space strengthens your magical bond.
- **Grow a Small Herb Garden:** Specifically with feline-friendly varieties like catnip or lemongrass. This allows you to harvest fresh herbs while providing your cat with a stimulating environment (supervised interaction is strongly recommended).

By embracing these methods, you can create a magical space that resonates with both you and your cat. Remember, the magic lies not just in the herbs or rituals, but in the deep connection you cultivate with your feline familiar.

Chapter 14: Feline Familiars Beyond Form: Sigils and Thoughtforms

The bond between the witch and the familiar transcends the physical realm. While the companionship of a living cat offers a powerful connection, some practitioners explore alternative avenues. This chapter delves into the creation of feline familiars through sigils and thoughtforms – magical constructs imbued with the essence of a cat. We'll explore the potential benefits and limitations of these extraordinary familiars, guiding you through the process of crafting your own feline companion in the astral plane.

Thoughtforms and Sigils: Giving Shape to Magic

Thoughtforms are non-physical energetic constructs created and sustained through focused intention and visualization. A feline thoughtform familiar can be a powerful tool for witches who struggle to find a suitable living cat due to allergies, living situations, or other limitations.

Here's how to create a feline thoughtform familiar:

- **Meditate on the Feline Archetype:** Focus on the qualities you associate with feline energy – independence, intuition, grace, and perhaps even a touch of mischief. Visualize these qualities embodied in the form of a cat.
- **Channel Your Intent:** Imbue your thought form with specific qualities you desire. Do you seek a protector? A guide for astral travel? A muse for creativity? Pour your focused intention into the visualization.
- **Sustain the Form:** Regular meditation and visualization exercises are key to maintaining the strength and coherence of your thoughtform familiar.

Sigils: A Feline Symbol for Focused Magic

Sigils are symbolic representations, often geometric designs, imbued with magical intent. A sigil representing a feline familiar can be used for focus, channeling energy, or as a bridge for communication with the feline archetype.

Here's how to create a feline sigil:

Crafting Your Feline Familiar Sigil: Unveiling Different Methods

The concept of a sigil, a symbol imbued with specific magical intent, offers a powerful way to connect with the essence of a feline familiar.

While the process can be tailored to your personal preferences, here are several popular methods for creating your own feline sigil:

1. The Sentence Method:

- **Start with a clear statement:** Define your desired qualities for your feline familiar. For example, "I call upon a spirit of feline protection" or "May this sigil channel the focus and agility of a cat."
- **Distill the essence:** Remove all vowels and repeating letters from your statement. This leaves you with a core set of consonants that hold the energetic essence of your intent.
- **Arrange and rearrange:** Write down the remaining letters and experiment with different combinations. Overlap them, create a geometric pattern, or use them as a starting point for a stylized drawing.
- **Refine and personalize:** As you experiment, a specific design will likely start to emerge. Refine it until you have a sigil that resonates with you and visually embodies your desired feline qualities.

2. Planetary and Astrological Correspondences:

- **Feline associations:** Research astrological and planetary associations with feline energy. For example, the Moon is often linked with intuition, a key feline trait.
- **Sigil creation through symbols:** Use symbols associated with these planets or stars to create your sigil. The crescent moon for the Moon, a glyph for Mars for fierceness, or a stylized eye for the Sun representing awareness are some options.
- **Combine and personalize:** Blend these symbols with other elements that resonate with you, creating a unique and personal sigil.

3. The Automatic Drawing Method:

- **Enter a relaxed state:** Meditate or engage in calming activities to quiet your mind and enter a receptive state.
- **Channel your intent:** Focus on the qualities you desire in your feline familiar.
- **Let your hand be guided:** With pen or pencil in hand, allow your hand to move freely on the paper without conscious control. Shapes and symbols may emerge that embody your feline essence.

- **Refine and interpret:** Once you have a drawing, analyze it and see if any specific symbols or shapes stand out. Refine these elements into a cohesive sigil design.

4. The Number Method:

This method utilizes numbers and a grid structure to create a sigil. Here's a step-by-step approach:

- **Assign numerical values:** Assign a number (1-9) to each letter of the alphabet. You can find many existing correspondences online or create your own intuitive associations.
- **Craft your phrase:** Form a statement that captures your desired qualities for your feline familiar. For instance, "Grant me the focus of a hunting cat" or "I call upon a spirit of feline protection."
- **Distill the essence:** Write down your phrase and remove all punctuation and spaces. Similar to the sentence method, eliminate any repeating letters. Now you have a core set of numbers representing your intent.
- **Create a grid:** Draw a 3x3 grid on a piece of paper.
- **Distribute the numbers:** Following a pattern (such as snake-like or spiral), add each number from your core set to a corresponding square in the grid. If a single-digit number appears multiple times, add them together and place the sum in a square. If the sum is a two-digit number, separate the digits and place them in individual squares.
- **For example:** If your phrase is "Grant me focus" and your letter correspondences are: G (7), R (2), A (1), N (5), T (4), M (3), E (5), F (6), O (6), and S (8), you'd remove duplicates and end up with 7, 2, 1, 5, 4, 3, and 8.
- **Analyze and design:** Once you have all the numbers placed within the grid, analyze the emerging squares. Are there any interesting lines or shapes created? Use these as a jumping-off point to design your sigil. You can draw lines connecting the squares, create a geometric pattern based on the numbers, or use the grid as a base for a more organic sigil design.

Consecration: Once you have your sigil, regardless of the method used, consecrate it through meditation or ritual. Imbue it with magical energy by focusing your intent and visualizing the sigil glowing with power. This activates your feline familiar sigil, making it a potent tool for connecting with feline energy in your magical practice.

Remember: There's no single "correct" way to create a sigil. Experiment with these methods, or develop your own unique approach. The key lies in focusing your intent and allowing your intuition to guide the design process. Once you have your sigil, consecrate it through meditation or ritual, imbuing it with magical energy.

By understanding the creation and use of both thought forms and sigils, you can extend the concept of a feline familiar beyond the physical realm. The journey continues as we explore the advantages and limitations of these magical companions in the following sections.

Utilizing Your Feline Familiar Construct: Focus, Channeling, and Communication

Once you've created your feline familiar sigil or thoughtform, it's time to explore how to integrate it into your magical practice.

Here's a breakdown of its potential uses and some key considerations:

Focus and Channeling:

- Meditate with your sigil or visualize your thoughtform to connect with its energy. During meditation, hold your sigil or close your eyes and visualize your thoughtform. Focus on the feline qualities you imbued it with – agility, intuition, independence. Feel the energy of these qualities flow through you, enhancing your own focus and magical abilities.
- Use it as a focal point for channeling feline-associated magical energies. When performing rituals or spells that require qualities like stealth, grace, or sharpened senses, use your sigil or thoughtform as a conduit. Visualize the sigil glowing with energy, or imagine your thoughtform beside you, amplifying the specific feline traits you wish to utilize.

Communication:

Developing a system of communication with your familiar construct can deepen your magical partnership.

Here are some methods to explore:

- **Interpret synchronicities:** Pay attention to coincidences that occur throughout your day, especially those related to feline symbolism. Seeing a black cat cross your path, encountering a feather, or even dreaming of a playful kitten could be messages from your familiar.
- **Use divination techniques:** Techniques like tarot or rune readings can be used to establish a dialogue with your familiar. Formulate a question related to your magical practice or personal life, then perform a reading while focusing on the energy of your familiar sigil or thoughtform.
- **Simply trust your intuition:** As you work with your familiar construct, you'll develop a deeper sense of its presence. Pay attention to gut feelings, sudden insights, or unexplainable urges – these could be subtle forms of communication from your familiar.

Limitations: Remember, a magical construct is not a living being.

While a sigil or thoughtform familiar can be a powerful tool, it's important to acknowledge its limitations. It lacks the independent sentience and complex emotional range of a physical cat. It won't offer companionship or unconditional love in the same way. However, by understanding its unique qualities, you can utilize your familiar construct to enhance your magical practice and cultivate a deeper connection with the essence of feline energy.

Here's a breakdown of its potential uses and some key considerations:

- **Accessibility:** For those who cannot have a physical cat, a magical construct familiar offers a way to connect with feline magic.
- **Living limitations:** Perhaps allergies, living situations, or other circumstances prevent you from having a physical cat. A sigil or thoughtform familiar can bridge this gap, allowing you to connect with the powerful energy of felines in your magical practice.
- **Exploration without commitment:** This method offers a safe way to explore the realm of feline magic before committing to the responsibility of caring for a living creature. You can experiment with channeling different feline traits and see how they resonate with your magical goals.
- **Focused Energy:** A sigil or thoughtform can be a powerful tool for channeling specific feline-associated energies in your magic.
- **Amplify your strengths:** Feel the need for more agility during your astral travels? Craft a sigil or thoughtform imbued with the essence of a leaping panther. Need to sharpen your intuition for divination? Visualize a wise, watchful owl as your familiar construct.
- **Tailor your magic:** The beauty of a magical construct familiar lies in its customizability. Focus on the specific feline qualities that align with your magical needs, creating a potent tool for channeling those energies into your spells and rituals.
- **Respectful Boundaries:** This method allows you to work with feline magic without the responsibility of caring for a living creature.
- **Respectful connection:** Some may not have the time or resources to care for a physical cat. A sigil or thoughtform familiar allows you to cultivate a magical connection with feline energy without infringing on the needs of a living being.
- **Balanced approach:** This method doesn't replace the irreplaceable bond with a living cat. If your circumstances allow, consider adopting a feline companion in the future. In the meantime, a magical construct familiar can be a stepping stone or a complementary practice alongside a physical feline friend.

By understanding these advantages and limitations, you can effectively utilize your feline familiar construct to enhance your magical practice and deepen your connection with the feline archetype.

Ethical Considerations: Working with the Feline Spirit

When creating and utilizing a feline-familiar construct, it's crucial to approach it with respect for the feline archetype:

- **Respect the Archetype:** Avoid creating a familiar that is subservient or disrespectful of the feline spirit. Strive for a partnership of mutual benefit. Imbue your familiar with the independent spirit and intelligence that defines feline nature.
- **Acknowledge the Limitations:** This is a magical construct, not a sentient being. It lacks the complex emotions and needs of a living cat. Treat it with respect as a tool for channeling feline energy, but avoid blurring the lines between the magical and the physical.

By understanding these advantages and limitations, you can effectively utilize your feline familiar construct to enhance your magical practice and deepen your connection with the feline archetype.

The Feline Familiar: A Magical Partnership

The concept of the familiar, a magical companion who walks beside the witch on their mystical path, holds a special place in feline lore. But the feline familiar transcends the physical realm. Whether you choose to forge a bond with a living cat or create a magical construct imbued with feline essence, the heart of this connection lies in the partnership you cultivate.

A physical feline companion offers an unparalleled experience. Their playful spirit, independent nature, and enigmatic gaze have captivated humans for millennia. These furry companions are more than just pets; they can be confidantes, protectors, and even muses. Their presence can soothe anxieties, heighten intuition, and inspire creativity. Through their playful pounces and watchful gazes, they can become a bridge between the mundane and the magical, reminding us to embrace the joy and wonder in the everyday world.

However, circumstances don't always allow for a living feline companion. Allergies, living situations, or travel restrictions may create limitations. Yet, the allure of feline magic remains. This is where the concept of the magical construct familiar takes hold. By crafting a sigil or thoughtform imbued with the essence of a cat, you can connect with feline energy in another way. This allows you to tap into the focus, agility, and intuition associated with felines, enriching your magical practice.

Whether your familiar is a living creature or a magical construct, the key lies in approaching this practice with respect, intention, and a deep appreciation for the feline spirit. Avoid creating a subservient familiar; strive for a partnership built on mutual respect and benefit. A living cat deserves a loving home, not a life dictated by magical servitude. A sigil or thoughtform, while a powerful tool, should not replace the irreplaceable bond with a furry friend.

When approached thoughtfully, the feline familiar, whether physical or magical, can become a potent ally on your magical journey. They offer companionship, guidance, and a unique connection to the unseen realms. Their playful spirit can remind you to approach life with a touch of whimsy, while their keen senses can guide you through the shadows. By fostering this connection, you create a magical partnership that purrs with power, enriching your craft and deepening your connection to the magic that flows through all living things.

Chapter 15: Cat-Inspired Scrying & Divination: Whispers from the Whiskered Ones

Cats have captivated humans for millennia, not just with their undeniable charm, but also with their enigmatic air and seemingly preternatural awareness. In many cultures, these furry familiars have been revered as oracles, possessing an uncanny ability to perceive the unseen and nudge us toward hidden truths.

This chapter dives into the fascinating world of cat-inspired scrying and divination. We'll explore ways to incorporate feline behavior and feline-inspired tools into your practice, transforming your cat's presence from a source of amusement into a wellspring of magical insights. Learn to interpret your feline companion's seemingly random actions as whispers from the whiskered ones, unlocking a deeper understanding of the world around you and the path ahead. Prepare to be surprised by the hidden messages your cat may be offering, and discover how to transform their playful antics and curious explorations into a potent form of divination.

Beyond Meows and Purrs: Interpreting Feline Signs

Deciphering the Dusty Bowl: The Language of the Litter Box

- Pay attention to changes in litter box habits (consistency, volume, location).
- Unusual patterns may indicate energetic shifts or a need to release negativity.
- Use your intuition and knowledge of your cat's usual habits to interpret the signs.

Feline Fascination: Unveiling Hidden Energies

- Observe what captures your cat's attention, especially persistent focus.
- Their fixation might reveal hidden energies in your home (cobwebs, drafts).
- The object of their interest could symbolize emotional blocks or areas for growth.
- By deciphering their focus, gain insights into your living space's energy.

The Playful Pendulum: A Feline Form of Divination

- Watch how your cat interacts with your pendulum.
- Their presence can influence pendulum movement, adding another layer of interpretation.
- A stop in the swing might signify a block, while a steady swing indicates a clear path.
- Playful batting could represent lightheartedness or a reminder to not be too serious.

By incorporating these and other feline-inspired techniques, you can transform your relationship with your cat into a powerful form of divination, enriching your magical practice and deepening your connection with your furry familiar.

Ethical Scrying with Catnip: Unlocking the Whispers of Your Feline Familiar

Catnip, that irresistible herb that sends felines into blissful zoomies, has a surprising history in divination practices.

Here's how to ethically incorporate it into your scrying rituals, creating a deeper connection with your cat and unlocking the subtle messages they offer:

Understanding Your Feline Oracle:

- **Respecting Individuality:** Not all cats are catnip enthusiasts! Just like us, they have varying preferences. Before incorporating catnip, observe your cat's natural behavior. If they show no interest, don't force it. There are plenty of other ways to connect with their energy during scrying.
- **Quality over Convenience:** When choosing catnip, prioritize organic options. This ensures it's safe for your feline friend to be around and free from harmful additives that might disrupt their behavior. Skip the brightly colored, commercially-produced toys – they often contain synthetic fillers that can be irritating or even toxic.

A Gentle Approach to Scrying:

- **Less is More:** Catnip's effects are potent but fleeting. Use a small amount during scrying sessions to avoid overwhelming your cat. A sprinkle on a natural fabric pouch or a pinch scattered near your scrying tool (like a crystal ball or bowl of water) is sufficient.
- **The Language of Behavior:** Focus on observing your cat's interaction with the catnip. Do they erupt in playful antics, suggesting a positive outlook for your inquiry? Or do they become mellow and cuddly, indicating a time for introspection and inner peace? Their behavior offers valuable insights into the energetic landscape surrounding your question.

Feline Familiars and the Tarot:

The bond between cats and humans is a mystical one. Many believe cats possess a natural sensitivity to psychic energy. During a tarot reading, observe if your cat shows a particular interest in a specific card. This might be a nudge from your feline familiar, offering a unique perspective on your situation. Consider the symbolism of the card they're drawn to – does it highlight a hidden aspect of your question or offer a lighter, more playful interpretation?

A Journey of Co-Creation:

Remember, these are just the stepping stones. The true magic lies in developing a personal practice of observation and interpretation. As you deepen your connection with your cat, you'll become more attuned to their subtle cues and the unique divinatory messages they offer. Scrying with catnip becomes a collaborative journey, where you learn to listen not just with your ears, but also with your heart and a keen eye for your feline friend's silent wisdom.

Feline-Inspired Divination Tools

Here are some ideas to enhance your cat-inspired divination practice:

- **Create a Feline-Themed Deck:** Craft your own tarot deck or oracle cards featuring cat imagery and symbolism. Imbue each card with the essence of a specific feline quality or behavior.
- **The Catnip Pouch:** Sew a small pouch filled with organic catnip. Hold it during divination rituals to invite feline intuition and guidance.
- **The Whisker Wand:** Find a fallen whisker from your cat. Attach it to a pendulum or dowsing rod as a unique tool for scrying and divination.

Always prioritize your cat's well-being. Their participation in your practice should be voluntary and enjoyable. By approaching cat-inspired divination with respect and a playful spirit, you can unlock a new dimension of communication with your feline familiar, transforming their purrs and playful antics into whispers of wisdom that guide you on your magical path.

Chapter 16: Feline Feng Shui: Creating Harmony for Cat and Craft

For witches who share their homes with feline companions, the concept of familiar goes far beyond the mystical realm. Our cats are furry housemates, confidantes, and sometimes, even mischievous participants in our magical endeavors.

But have you ever considered how your living space itself can influence the well-being of both you and your feline familiar? This chapter dives into the fascinating world of Feline Feng Shui, exploring ways to integrate the ancient practice of harmonizing energy flow into a living space that caters to both your cat's needs and your magical practice. By creating a home environment that strengthens comfort and joy for all inhabitants, both human and feline, you can create a sense of peace, purpose, and perhaps even a touch of extra magic in your everyday life.

The Feline Perspective: A Cat-Centric Approach

Cats, with their keen senses and sensitivity to energy, have their own unique preferences for their environment. By incorporating these feline Feng Shui principles, you can create a haven that caters to their natural instincts and fosters a sense of security and well-being.

Here's how to craft a space that's both magically potent and purr-fectly suited to your feline familiar:

Vertical Territory: A Throne Above It All:
- **Cat Trees & Shelves:** Incorporate cat trees, shelves, or climbing structures positioned around the room, allowing them to claim their vertical territory.
- **Magical Sigils:** As you install these vertical elements, imbue them with intention, perhaps symbolizing protection, dominance, or a watchful eye.

Command Centers: A View Fit for Royalty

- **Window Perches:** Provide window perches that allow your cat to survey their domain and observe the natural world outside.
- **Strategic Placement:** Place strategically placed cat beds with soft blankets in areas with good views, creating personal command centers.
- **Natural Stimulation:** Consider placing these perches near windows that overlook natural elements like trees or birds, further stimulating their instincts and enriching their environment.

Clear Pathways: Freedom to Roam

- **Unobstructed Movement:** Ensure clear pathways throughout your home so your cat can navigate freely without feeling cornered.
- **Decluttering:** Avoid clutter that might obstruct their movement, and consider rearranging furniture to create designated walkways.
- **Energy Flow:** A cat who feels safe and secure in their ability to move freely is more likely to be relaxed and open to energetic harmonies.

Stimulating Zones: Playgrounds for Positive Energy

- **Designated Play Areas:** Place scratching posts and interactive toys in designated areas.
- **Toy Rotation:** Rotate toys regularly to keep your cat engaged and prevent them from resorting to scratching furniture.
- **Channeling Energy:** As your cat engages with the toys, focus on channeling vital energy and joyful vibrations into the space during your magical rituals.

Harmony for Human and Familiar:

Creating a shared space for your magical practice and your feline familiar requires a touch of compromise and creativity.

Here's how to strike a balance between your needs and your cat's:

The Altar Space: Sharing the Sacred

- **Calm and Clutter-Free:** Designate a sacred space for your magical practice. Ideally, this should be a calm and clutter-free area, conducive to focusing your energy.
- **Feline-Friendly Touches:** Consider incorporating elements that appeal to your cat as well. A scratching post or a comfy bed placed strategically near your altar (but not directly on it) can encourage their presence without disrupting the energy. This allows your familiar to be a part of your practice without interfering with the tools or flow of your rituals.

Elemental Balance: A Symbiotic Symphony

The Five Elements: The five elements of Feng Shui – wood, fire, earth, metal, and water – can be used to create harmony in your shared space. Consider incorporating these elements in ways that benefit both you and your cat.

- **Wood:** Think live plants (safe for cats!), wooden furniture, or woven baskets for cat toys. These elements represent growth and new beginnings, while also providing enrichment for your feline friend.
- **Fire:** Candles (kept safely out of paw-reach, or alternatively use LED candles) or strategically placed lamps can represent the fire element in your practice. Catnip toys (used sparingly and ethically) can also add a touch of fiery energy while stimulating your cat's playful side.
- **Earth:** Crystals and stones can represent the earth element, but ensure they're kept out of reach or displayed in enclosed cases. Consider using calming cat litter or placing a designated digging area with earth-toned pebbles to fulfill your cat's natural digging instincts.
- **Metal:** Metal chimes or wind instruments can represent the metal element in your Feng Shui practice. Food and water bowls made from stainless steel can fulfill this purpose as well, providing a practical and visually appealing option that caters to your cat's needs.
- **Water:** A water fountain can be a source of hydration for your cat while representing the water element in your Feng Shui practice. Choose a design that's both aesthetically pleasing and encourages your cat to drink safely from the flowing water.

Crystal Considerations: Safety First

- **Toxic Beauty:** While crystals can enhance your magical practice, some are toxic to cats. Keep crystals out of reach or enclosed in display cases to avoid any potential accidents. **Here's a list of crystals to absolutely avoid having around your feline friend:**
  Bornite (Peacock Ore)
  Cinnabar (Mercury Sulfide)
  Malachite
  Any crystal that is chipped, cracked, or can be broken into small pieces (These pose a choking hazard)
- **Tumbled Stone Alternatives:** Consider using tumbled stones in pouches you wear during rituals, ensuring your cat has no access to these potentially harmful objects.

Calming Scents: A Shared Tranquility

- **Herbal Harmony:** Certain herbs like catnip (used safely and ethically) or valerian root (kept out of your cat's reach) can create a tranquil environment. Place them strategically in designated areas to promote relaxation for both you and your cat. Catnip can be used in small amounts in pouches near your altar during rituals, while valerian root can be diffused in a safe location that your cat cannot access.

Feline Feng Shui in Action:

Here are some examples of how to integrate feline needs with your magical practice, creating a harmonious flow of energy for both you and your whiskered companion:

Consecrate Climbing Structures:

- **Cleanse and bless:** Use smoke from cleansing herbs like sage or mugwort to clear away any stagnant energy.
- **Infuse with positive energy:** Follow the cleansing with a blessing or visualization. Imagine the structure pulsating with an energetic light that resonates with scratching and climbing.
- **Irresistible playground:** This positive energy creates an irresistible playground for your feline friend, keeping them away from your furniture.

Charge Toys with Intention:

- **Imbue before playtime:** Before engaging in playtime with your cat, imbue their toys with positive intentions.
- **Visualize energetic light:** Hold the toy in your hands and visualize it pulsating with an energetic light.
- **Focus your intent:** Depending on your desired outcome, focus your intent on vitality, agility, or playful energy.

- **Enhanced tendencies:** As your cat engages with the charged toy, they'll be absorbing this energy, enhancing their natural tendencies.

Meditation with Your Familiar:

- **Create a comfortable space:** Create a meditation space that includes a comfortable spot for your cat.
- **Options:** This could be a dedicated meditation cushion with a soft blanket placed nearby or a designated sunbeam on the floor.
- **Grounding force:** As you practice mindfulness, their presence can be a grounding force.
- **Deeper meditation:** Their rhythmic breathing and calming purrs can help you settle into a deeper state of meditation.
- **Peace and connection:** This fosters a sense of peace and connection for both you and your feline friend.

Remember: The goal is to create a harmonious space that celebrates the unique bond you share with your feline companion. By incorporating elements that cater to both your cat's needs and your magical practice, you foster a sense of well-being for all inhabitants and create a truly magical home.

Chapter 17: Whiskered Wisdom in Action - Sample Spells for the Feline Familiar

The witch's familiar—a creature imbued with intuition and power, forming an unshakeable bond with its companion. But this connection extends far beyond the physical realm. In the paws of a feline familiar lies a potent wellspring of magic, waiting to be tapped into.

This chapter dives into the secrets of incorporating feline energy into your witchcraft practice. We'll explore six sample spells, each drawing upon the unique qualities associated with cats. These spells will enrich your craft, fostering a deeper connection with your familiar and unlocking the potential that lies within your purrfect companion.

Here are six sample spells, drawing upon the unique qualities associated with cats, to enrich your craft:

Spell of Confidence and Grace (For Job Interviews or Presentations):

Ingredients:

- ☐ A pinch of catnip (ethically sourced)

- [ ] A white candle
- [ ] A Pinch of rosemary (associated with memory and focus)
- [ ] A small piece of paper

Process:

1. Light the white candle, symbolizing clarity and focus.
2. Hold the catnip in your hands, infusing it with your intention of confidence and grace.
3. Think about a time you witnessed your cat exhibiting these qualities.
4. Mentally transfer this feline energy into the catnip.
5. Place the rosemary and the catnip on the piece of paper.
6. As you fold the paper into a small pouch, whisper your intention for success in the upcoming interview or presentation.
7. Tuck the pouch into your pocket or bra, close to your body, throughout the event.
8. Visualize your cat embodying confidence and grace.
9. Imagine their steady gaze and unwavering presence supporting you.

Protection Charm for Travelers (For Safe Journeys):

Ingredients:

- [ ] A black feather (molted naturally, never plucked)
- [ ] A pinch of mugwort (associated with protection)
- [ ] A sprig of lavender (associated with peace)
- [ ] A small travel pouch.

Process:

1. Cleanse the feather with incense smoke or moonlight.
2. Hold the mugwort and lavender in your hands, infusing them with your intention for a safe journey.
3. Think about your cat's keen senses and awareness, their ability to navigate their environment with confidence.
4. Channel this feline energy into the herbs.
5. Place the feather, mugwort, and lavender into the travel pouch.
6. Whenever you feel anxious during your travels, hold the pouch and visualize your cat as a guardian, keeping you safe on your journey.
7. Imagine your cat perched high up, surveying the landscape with watchful eyes. Feel their presence as a source of protection during your travels.

Healing Spell for a Beloved Companion (For Animals or Humans):

Ingredients:

- ☐ A healing crystal (such as amethyst or rose quartz)
- ☐ Calming catnip (used sparingly and ethically)
- ☐ A soft cloth

Process:

1. Cleanse the crystal with your preferred method.
2. Place the crystal on your pet (or on yourself if healing yourself) and focus on your intention for healing and well-being.
3. Visualize white light emanating from the crystal, infusing your companion with restorative energy.
4. Gently stroke the area with the soft cloth infused with calming catnip, mimicking the soothing purr and touch of your feline familiar.
5. Think about the rhythmic purring of your cat, a sound often associated with healing.
6. Channel this purring energy into your touch and the crystal.

Calming Spell for Anxious Times (For Relaxation and Stress Relief):

Ingredients:

- ☐ Dried chamomile flowers (associated with relaxation)
- ☐ A blue candle (associated with peace and tranquility)
- ☐ A comfortable blanket or resting place for your cat.

Process:

1. Light the blue candle in a safe space.
2. Scatter the chamomile flowers around the candle or place them in a pouch nearby.
3. Create a comfortable space for your cat to rest, near the calming blue light and the chamomile scent.
4. Sit or lie down near your cat, focusing on their slow, rhythmic breathing.
5. Allow their tranquility to wash over you, mirroring their relaxed state.
6. Observe your cat's slow blinks and relaxed posture. Mentally connect with their peaceful energy and allow it to soothe your own anxieties.

Creativity Spell with Feline Inspiration (For Writers, Artists, or Anyone Seeking Creative Flow):

Ingredients:

- [ ] A feather pen (or writing utensil of choice)
- [ ] A pinch of catnip (used ethically)
- [ ] A citrine crystal (associated with creativity)
- [ ] A small piece of paper

Process:

1. Hold the feather pen and the citrine crystal, infusing them with your intention for creative inspiration.
2. Think about your cat's moments of playfulness and their curious exploration of the world. Channel this feline energy of curiosity and discovery into the pen and crystal.
3. Light some incense (such as lavender or sandalwood) to clear the space and enhance focus. On the piece of paper, write down a phrase or question to spark your creativity.
4. Hold the pen, feeling the infused energy, and begin to write or create, allowing your imagination to flow freely like your playful feline companion.
5. Visualize your cat batting at a toy or chasing a butterfly, their enthusiasm and focus fueling your own creative spark.

Spell of Intuition and Hidden Messages (For Divination and Guidance):

Ingredients:

- [ ] A moonstone (associated with intuition)
- [ ] A small pouch
- [ ] A pinch of catnip (used ethically)
- [ ] A pen and paper

Process:

1. Cleanse the moonstone with moonlight or running water.
2. Hold the moonstone and the catnip, focusing your intention on receiving clear messages and insights.
3. Think about your cat's keen senses and ability to pick up on subtle cues.
4. Channel this feline intuition into the moonstone and the catnip.
5. Place the moonstone in the pouch with the catnip.

6. Before sleep or during meditation, hold the pouch and ask a question you seek guidance on. Write down any dreams, visions, or intuitive feelings that arise.
7. Imagine your cat staring intently at something unseen, their whiskers twitching.
8. Trust that their heightened awareness is guiding you toward the answers you seek.

Remember: These are just a starting point. Feel free to experiment with these spells, substitute ingredients based on your needs and preferences, and personalize them to reflect your unique bond with your feline familiar. As you work with these spells and deepen your connection with your cat, the magic you create together will become even more potent and meaningful.

Chapter 18: Exploring Feline Astrology: Traits and Alignments

Forget chasing yarn balls, our feline friends are secretly celestial beings! This chapter explores the fascinating world of feline astrology. We'll purr-use the mysteries of the zodiac to unravel connections between a cat's breed, personality, and astrological twin. Uncover the magical associations of your "astrological feline" and discover how to work with their cosmic energy to enhance your witchcraft practice.

Is Feline Astrology Real?

Feline astrology is not a formally recognized astrological system. However, it serves as a playful and insightful lens through which we can explore the fascinating connection between cats and the cosmos. While not a definitive science, it offers a framework for understanding our feline companions on a deeper level. By considering your cat's breed, personality traits, and even their birthday, you can identify potential alignments with specific astrological signs. These alignments can offer valuable clues about your cat's motivations, energy levels, and how they might interact with the world around them.

Is your cat a regal and independent Maine Coon with a penchant for sunbeams? Perhaps they share a connection with Leo, the sign associated with confidence and leadership. On the other hand, a mischievous Siamese with a boundless curiosity might resonate more with Gemini, the sign of the twins, known for their playful nature and love of exploration. Remember, feline astrology is a fun and flexible system. Don't be afraid to let your intuition guide you as you explore the unique personality of your whiskered companion.

Matching Breeds and Personalities to Signs:

Here's a glimpse into some potential feline-astrological pairings:

- **Fire Signs (Aries, Leo, Sagittarius):** These fiery felines are like their astrological counterparts – energetic, playful, and independent. Breeds like Siamese, Bengals, and Abyssinian cats often exhibit these traits. Fire signs are associated with leadership, passion, and creativity. In your magical practice, consider incorporating fire elements like candles or exploring rituals focused on confidence and inspiration, potentially involving your fiery feline familiar.
- **Earth Signs (Taurus, Virgo, Capricorn):** These grounded cats are like their earth sign counterparts – practical, cautious, and routine-oriented. Breeds like Persians, Maine Coons, and Sphynx cats often embody these qualities. Earth signs are associated with stability, practicality, and abundance. You can work with your earth sign cat in rituals focused on grounding, protection, or manifesting material desires.
- **Air Signs (Gemini, Libra, Aquarius):** These social butterflies are like their air sign counterparts – curious, communicative, and adaptable. Breeds like Oriental Shorthairs, Burmese, and Cornish Rex cats often exhibit these traits. Air signs are associated with communication, intellect, and social connections. Consider incorporating air elements like incense or feathers in your practice. Your air sign cat might be a great companion during meditations focused on mental clarity or divination rituals.
- **Water Signs (Cancer, Scorpio, Pisces):** These deeply emotional cats are like their water sign counterparts – sensitive, intuitive, and sometimes mysterious. Breeds like Ragdolls, Russian Blues, and Bombay cats often embody these qualities. Water signs are associated with emotions, intuition, and psychic abilities. You can work with your water sign cat in rituals focused on emotional healing, dreamwork, or connecting with your intuition.

Remember: These are just starting points. Observing your cat's unique personality is key. A playful and cuddly Maine Coon might have a fire sign influence despite its breed, channeling their inner Leo with bursts of energy and regal air.

Conversely, a sleek Siamese radiating an aura of mystery could surprise you with a strong connection to a water sign, possessing a deep emotional intelligence and a penchant for introspection. Don't be afraid to look beyond breed stereotypes and delve into your cat's individual quirks. Their true astrological feline might just surprise you, offering even deeper insights into their magical potential and strengthening the bond you share within your witchcraft practice.

Deeper Understanding of Your Cat:

By considering your cat's astrological alignment, you can gain a deeper understanding of their:

- **Motivations:** Is your cat a cuddle monster or a fearless explorer? Their astrological sign can offer clues about what drives their behavior. For instance, a Leo cat might crave attention and playtime, while a Virgo cat might seek out quiet routines and dedicated scratching areas.
- **Preferences:** Understanding your cat's element (fire, earth, air, water) can help you tailor their environment to their liking. Fire sign cats might appreciate sunny window perches, while water sign cats might prefer cozy hideaways.
- **Communication Style:** Does your cat meow incessantly or express affection through subtle head bumps? Their astrological sign can shed light on how they communicate. Air sign cats might be very vocal, while earth sign cats might show their love through gentle grooming or purring.

Enhanced Magical Partnership:

Understanding your cat's astrological energy can help you create magical practices that resonate with both of you:

- **Shared Rituals:** Fire sign cats might enjoy playful wand exercises or energetic visualization rituals. Earth sign cats might find comfort in rituals focused on grounding and protection, incorporating herbs like lavender or mugwort.
- **Elemental Correspondences:** Align your magical workings with your cat's element. Water sign cats might be particularly receptive to moon magic, while air sign cats might excel at amplifying the power of your intentions.
- **Strengthening the Bond:** Sharing magical experiences can deepen the connection with your feline familiar.

A Fun and Insightful Exploration:

Feline astrology is a playful way to explore the connection between cats, the cosmos, and your own magical practice:

- **Beyond Breeds:** Move past breed stereotypes. A laid-back Persian might have a surprising connection to a water sign, while a mischievous Sphynx could embody the air sign's love of intellectual stimulation.
- **Personalized Insights:** Feline astrology offers a unique lens to understand your cat's individual quirks and personality.
- **A Framework for Exploration:** This playful system allows you to explore the potential magical associations your cat might have, enriching your witchcraft practice.

Working with Your Feline Familiar Based on Their Alignment:

Fire Signs (Aries, Leo, Sagittarius):

- **Encourage Playful Energy:** Provide interactive toys, engage in wand play, or create agility courses.
- **Energetic Rituals:** Incorporate fire elements like candles or crystals like carnelian into your rituals.
- **Waxing Moon Magic:** Fire sign cats might be particularly receptive to magical workings during waxing moons, a time of increased energy.

Earth Signs (Taurus, Virgo, Capricorn):

- **Stable and Predictable Environment:** Provide a consistent routine, designated scratching areas, and familiar hiding spots.
- **Herbal Remedies:** Explore calming herbal remedies like chamomile or catnip to promote relaxation.
- **Grounding and Protection Rituals:** Earth sign cats might find comfort in rituals focused on grounding and protection, incorporating elements like crystals like black tourmaline or smoky quartz.

Air Signs (Gemini, Libra, Aquarius):

- **Engage Their Curiosity:** Offer puzzle feeders, rotate toys regularly, and provide stimulating environments.
- **Divination and Knowledge-Seeking:** These cats might excel as companions during divination rituals like tarot readings or meditations focused on expanding your knowledge.
- **Mental Stimulation:** Air sign cats might appreciate clicker training or learning simple tricks to keep their minds sharp.

Water Signs (Cancer, Scorpio, Pisces):

- **Safe and Nurturing Space:** Create a calm and predictable environment with plenty of cozy hideaways.
- **Emotional Healing:** Water sign cats might be drawn to rituals focused on emotional healing or dream interpretation, incorporating calming elements like water or moonstone crystals.
- **Intuition and Empathy:** These highly intuitive cats might be especially sensitive to your emotions and energy.

Always prioritize your cat's well-being. Never force them to participate in any activities that cause them stress or discomfort. Their comfort and happiness should always come first.

Feline Astrology: A Journey of Discovery

Exploring feline astrology is a journey of discovery. By observing your cat, considering their astrological alignment, and incorporating their unique energy into your practice, you can deepen your bond with your feline familiar and create a truly magical partnership. This playful exploration unlocks hidden aspects of your cat's personality, fostering a deeper understanding and appreciation for their subtle cues and enigmatic nature. Ultimately, feline astrology becomes a bridge between your human world and your cat's celestial connection, enriching your witchcraft practice and strengthening the purrfect bond you share.

Chapter 19: Dreamweaving with Your Feline Familiar

Cats have long captivated our imaginations, their silent steps and enigmatic gaze hinting at a connection to unseen realms. Perhaps it's no surprise then, that these furry companions have been revered as guardians of the dreamscape for centuries. This chapter dives into the fascinating world of dreamweaving with your feline familiar.

We'll explore techniques for fostering a deeper connection with your cat in the dream world, learning to decipher the hidden messages and potent magic they offer within the ethereal realm. Prepare to unlock the secrets whispered on moonlit nights, and embark on a journey of shared dreamscapes with your purrfect companion.

The Feline Dream Guide:

Cats possess an acute awareness of the unseen, often flitting between slumber and wakefulness with ease. They can be powerful guides in the dreamscape, offering insights into your subconscious mind and illuminating your magical path. By fostering a conscious connection with your cat during sleep, you can unlock a wealth of knowledge and intuition, transforming your dreams into a potent tool for self-discovery and magical growth.

Before Embarking on Your Dreamweaving Journey:

Before diving into the magical world of dream weaving with your feline familiar, please consider these steps to prepare the ground and strengthen your connection:

- **Strengthen Your Bond:** In the waking world, lay the foundation for dream encounters. Spend quality time playing, cuddling, and simply observing your cat's behavior. This fosters a deep sense of trust and communication, making it more likely you'll connect with them in the dreamscape. Pay attention to their subtle cues and quirks – these could become potent symbols within your dreams.
- **Set Your Intention:** Before drifting off to sleep, plant a seed of intention in your mind. Visualize your cat waiting for you in your dreamscape, ready to act as your guide. Imagine the specific message or insight you seek, or the aspect of your magical path you wish to illuminate. Writing down your intention in a dedicated dream journal can further solidify your focus and increase the chances of a vivid encounter.
- **Create a Dream-Friendly Environment:** Transform your sleep space into a haven for dream recall. Ensure it's free from distractions and clutter, promoting a sense of peace and tranquility. Incorporate calming scents like lavender or chamomile to ease your mind and body into a restful state. Consider placing a soft blanket or familiar toy belonging to your cat near your bedside – a bridge between your waking world and the dreamscape they inhabit.

Techniques for Dreamweaving:

Unveiling the secrets whispered on moonlit nights requires fostering a deeper connection with your feline familiar in the dream world. Here are some techniques to embark on your dream weaving journey:

- **Lucid Dreaming:** Cultivate the ability to become aware that you are dreaming while still asleep. This lucidity allows you to interact with the dreamscape and potentially encounter your feline familiar. Explore techniques like the Wake Back To Bed (WBTB) method, where you set an alarm to wake yourself after a few hours of sleep and then return to bed with the intention of lucid dreaming. Incorporating reality checks throughout the day, like questioning the solidity of walls or looking at your hands, can also train your mind to recognize dream signs.
- **Dream Incubation:** Before sleep, focus on a specific question or intention related to your magical path or personal growth. Visualize your cat as a guide, waiting for you in the dreamscape and ready to offer answers or insights. Repeating this visualization and writing down your intention in a dream journal can further solidify your focus and increase the chances of encountering your familiar with a message or symbol relevant to your inquiry.
- **Shared Dream Rituals:** Create a pre-sleep ritual to strengthen the energetic bridge between you and your feline companion. This could involve gentle massage with calming essential oils like lavender, reciting a mantra focused on dream recall, or leaving a

favorite toy of your cat near your bedside. As you drift off, visualize your cat waiting for you in your dreamscape, ready to embark on a shared adventure.

- **Dream Interpretation:** Upon waking, record your dreams in detail, paying close attention to any feline symbolism or encounters. Even fleeting appearances of your cat can hold significant meaning. Consider the emotional tone of the dream, any actions your cat took, and the overall context of the dreamscape. By referencing dream dictionaries and reflecting on your waking life experiences, you can begin to decipher the hidden messages and guidance offered by your feline familiar.

Interpreting Dreams with Your Cat:

Unveiling the messages woven into your dream encounters with your feline familiar requires close attention to detail. Here are some key considerations:

- **Cat's Behavior:** Is your cat playful and energetic, mirroring your own creative spark, or are they calm and watchful, perhaps urging you to observe a situation with more focus? Their behavior might reflect an aspect of your own energy or emotions that needs attention. A particularly aggressive or withdrawn cat could symbolize hidden anxieties or a need for boundaries.
- **Cat's Appearance:** Does your cat appear healthy and vibrant, mirroring your own sense of well-being, or are they injured or malnourished? The cat's physical state could symbolize aspects of your own physical or emotional health. A limping cat might suggest a need to slow down and address an injury, while a sleek and powerful feline could represent feelings of empowerment.
- **Dream Setting:** Are you in a familiar location with your cat, like your cozy living room, suggesting a focus on domestic matters, or a fantastical dreamscape filled with fantastical creatures, hinting at a journey of self-discovery? The setting can offer clues about the themes or messages of the dream. Exploring a lush forest with your cat might symbolize personal growth and connection to nature while encountering them in a crowded marketplace could represent challenges in navigating social situations.

Working with Your Dreams:

Understanding the messages delivered by your feline familiar requires dedicated dream work. Here are some practices to integrate into your journey:

- **Dream Journaling:** Upon waking, immediately record your dreams in a dedicated journal, capturing as much detail as possible, especially your interactions with your cat. Write down the emotions you felt in the dream, the actions your cat took, and any specific symbols or imagery that stood out. Over time, you may identify recurring themes or messages that offer valuable insights into your subconscious mind and magical path.

- **Symbolism and Archetypes:** Research dream symbolism and archetypes to gain a deeper understanding of the elements in your dreams, including the presence of your cat. Consider the cultural and personal associations you have with cats. For example, a black cat might symbolize mystery or hidden aspects of yourself, while a white cat could represent purity or new beginnings. By layering these interpretations with your own intuition, you can unlock a richer understanding of your feline familiar's dream messages.

Safety and Boundaries:

Respecting the energetic connection with your feline familiar is paramount in dream weaving. Here are some key safety considerations:

- **Respect Your Cat's Boundaries:** Just as in the waking world, respect your cat's boundaries within the dreamscape. If they appear hesitant to interact, don't force the encounter. This could indicate they're not ready to communicate a particular message or that your own emotional state might be creating a barrier.
- **Maintain a Positive Focus:** While dreams can be unsettling at times, particularly if they touch on anxieties or unresolved issues, maintain a positive attitude and focus on the guidance your cat offers. Even seemingly negative dream messages can be interpreted as opportunities for growth and transformation. By approaching your dreams with an open mind and a sense of trust in your feline companion, you can navigate them with confidence and gain valuable insights.
- **Grounding Techniques:** If a dream encounter becomes overwhelming, employ grounding techniques to bring yourself back to a centered and safe space. Visualize a white light surrounding you, imagine yourself stepping back from the dreamscape, or repeat a calming mantra such as "I am safe, I am loved, I am protected."
- **Wake Up if Necessary:** If a dream ever feels truly frightening or out of control, you have the power to wake yourself up. Simply setting the intention to awaken before sleep can empower you to take control of the dreamscape if necessary.

Dream weaving with Your Feline Familiar: A Path to Self-Discovery

By fostering a connection with your cat in the dreamscape, you start a journey of self-discovery that extends far beyond the realm of sleep. Your feline familiar can act as a bridge to your subconscious mind, offering invaluable insights into your intuition, creativity, and the hidden aspects of your magical path. As you explore the dreamscape together, your bond deepens, and the magic you create transcends the boundaries of the waking world.

The messages in your dream encounters can illuminate emotional blockages, guide you toward untapped potential, and reveal hidden truths about yourself and your magical practice. With each shared dream adventure, you learn to decipher the subtle cues and symbolism your cat offers, fostering a deeper understanding of their enigmatic nature. This newfound awareness enriches your waking relationship, strengthening the purrfect partnership you share.

Dreamweaving with your cat is not just about interpreting symbols or achieving lucidity; it's about cultivating deeper trust and communication with your feline companion. As you learn to navigate the dreamscape together, a sense of shared purpose and understanding blossoms. This newfound connection empowers you to tap into a potent source of magical energy, one that flows freely between you and your familiar, enriching your witchcraft practice and amplifying your intentions.

So, the next time you drift off to sleep, invite your feline friend to join you on your dream journey. With a gentle touch, a shared purr, and a whispered message in the ethereal realm, your cat can become your most trusted guide, leading you on a path of self-discovery and unlocking the magic that lies within.

Chapter 20: Creating Feline Potions and Remedies (Ethical and Herbal)

The bond between the witch and familiar transcends the physical world, extending into the realm of healing and well-being. This chapter delves into the fascinating world of crafting safe and ethical herbal remedies specifically designed to support your feline companion's health. We'll explore a variety of natural ingredients with properties that can soothe upset tummies, promote relaxation, or gently address minor ailments.

However, it's crucial to remember that these remedies are intended to be complementary, not a substitute for professional veterinary care. Always consult your veterinarian for any serious health concerns your cat might have.

This chapter empowers you to become a proactive partner in your cat's well-being, offering gentle herbal solutions alongside the expertise of your trusted vet.

So, grab your mortar and pestle, gather your favorite feline friend (with a healthy dose of caution!), and get ready to explore the wonderful world of crafting natural remedies for your purrfect companion!

The Feline Herbalist's Toolkit:

Before diving into the delightful world of crafting herbal remedies for your feline familiar, here are some essential considerations to ensure the safety and well-being of your furry friend:

- **Ethical Sourcing:** As a witch and a cat guardian, responsible sourcing is paramount. Support reputable vendors who prioritize sustainable harvesting and ethical sourcing practices for their herbs. Look for certifications like organic or fair trade whenever possible. This ensures the quality of the ingredients you'll be using and minimizes your environmental impact.
- **Feline-Friendly Herbs:** It's important to remember that many herbs beneficial for humans can be toxic or harmful to cats. Their smaller bodies and unique metabolisms process substances differently. Do thorough research to ensure the chosen herbs are safe for feline consumption. Consult reputable herbal resources specifically designed for cats, and never hesitate to consult your veterinarian if you have any questions.
- **Dosage and Dilution:** Cats have a much smaller body mass than humans. Always prioritize safety by using diluted concentrations of herbs when crafting remedies for your feline companion. There's a big difference between a human cup of chamomile tea and a safe dose for your cat. Utilize resources that provide safe dosage information specifically for cats, and remember, less is always more when it comes to herbal remedies for your furry friend.
- **Start Low, Monitor Closely:** When introducing a new herbal remedy to your cat, it's crucial to start with a very low dose and monitor their reaction closely. Look for any signs of discomfort, such as vomiting, diarrhea, or loss of appetite. If you notice any adverse reactions, discontinue use immediately and consult your veterinarian.

Feline Potions and Remedies:

Calming Catnip Tincture:

Ingredients:

- ☐ Dried catnip (ethically sourced)
- ☐ High-proof vodka (grain alcohol)
- ☐ Glass dropper bottle

Process:

1. Fill a clean jar ¾ full with dried catnip.
2. Cover with vodka, ensuring all the catnip is submerged.
3. Seal the jar tightly and store it in a cool, dark place for 4-6 weeks, shaking occasionally.
4. Strain the tincture into a glass dropper bottle, discarding the plant material.

5. Compost the leftover catnip if possible.

Uses:

- Dilute a few drops of the tincture in water and offer it to your cat in a shallow dish. This can be particularly helpful during stressful situations like thunderstorms or fireworks.

Disclaimer: Start with a minimal dose and observe your cat's reaction. Catnip affects cats differently, and some may not respond positively.

Stress-Relieving Lavender Spray:

Ingredients:

- ☐ Dried lavender flowers
- ☐ Witch hazel (alcohol-free)
- ☐ Distilled water
- ☐ Spray bottle

Process:

1. Steep 1 tablespoon of dried lavender flowers in 1 cup of boiling water for 10-15 minutes.
2. Strain the cooled liquid and discard the plant material.
3. Compost the leftover lavender if possible.
4. Combine the lavender infusion with 1 cup of witch hazel in a spray bottle.
5. Shake well before use.

Uses:

- Lightly mist your cat's bedding or resting area with the lavender spray to create a calming environment.

Disclaimer: Avoid spraying directly on your cat, as they might ingest it while grooming.

Digestive Support Herbal Blend:

Ingredients:

- ☐ Dried slippery elm bark (powdered)
- ☐ Dried chamomile flowers

☐ Organic oat bran

Process:

1. Combine equal parts of each ingredient in a small bowl.
2. Store in an airtight container in a cool, dark place.

Uses:

- Sprinkle a small amount of the herbal blend onto your cat's wet food or a small amount of water. This can be helpful for occasional digestive discomfort.

Disclaimer: Discontinue use if your cat experiences any diarrhea or vomiting.

Respiratory Support Herbal Blend:

Ingredients:

☐ Dried elderflower (dried, not fresh)
☐ Dried echinacea (powdered)
☐ Organic slippery elm bark (powdered)

Process:

1. Combine equal parts of each ingredient in a small bowl.
2. Store in an airtight container in a cool, dark place.

Uses:

- Sprinkle a small amount of the herbal blend onto your cat's wet food or a small amount of water. This can be helpful for mild respiratory discomfort.

Disclaimer:

- **Discontinue use if your cat experiences any difficulty breathing or worsening symptoms.**
- These are just a few examples. There are many other herbs with potential benefits for feline health.
- **Always research thoroughly before using any new herb and consult with a veterinarian if unsure.**

Beyond the Potions: Holistic Care for Your Feline Familiar

Consider these additional practices:

- **Healthy Diet:** Provide your cat with a high-quality diet appropriate for their age and activity level. Research different food options and consult your veterinarian to find the best fit for your cat. Consider a mix of wet and dry food to provide hydration and variety.
- **Fresh Water:** Ensure your cat has access to clean, fresh water at all times. Cats can be picky drinkers, so try using a wider water bowl or a water fountain to entice them.
- **Regular Exercise:** Engage your cat in daily playtime to stimulate their body and mind. Rotate through a variety of toys to keep things interesting, and consider interactive toys that mimic hunting or chasing prey. Short bursts of play throughout the day are ideal.
- **Clean Environment:** Maintain a clean litter box and a tidy living space to reduce stress for your cat. Scoop the litter box at least once a day, and completely change the litter regularly. Provide multiple litter boxes in different locations, especially in multi-cat households. Keep your home clutter-free by creating designated scratching areas and climbing spaces for your cat.
- **Mental Stimulation:** In addition to physical exercise, provide mental stimulation for your cat. Train them with simple tricks, hide treats or catnip toys for them to find, or rotate their climbing structures and scratching posts. Window perches can offer endless entertainment as they watch the world go by.

Chapter 21: Feline Familiars and Shadow Work: Facing Your Inner Panther

If you're curious about the power of self-discovery, you might enjoy my previous book, Embracing The Witch's Shadow. We explore the transformative practice of shadow work – uncovering the hidden aspects of ourselves, the emotions we've pushed aside, and the desires we've kept under wraps. This chapter explores how your feline familiar can be a powerful guide on this often challenging yet ultimately liberating journey.

Cats, with their independent spirits and untamed instincts, can act as mirrors to our own shadow selves. Their playful swats and midnight yowls might tap into our buried aggression or unacknowledged wildness. Their aloof independence can challenge our need for control, while their moments of intense cuddling might highlight our hidden vulnerability.

Shadow Work with Your Feline Familiar:

Here's how your cat can be an invaluable companion in shadow work:

Shadow Reflections in Feline Behavior:

Playfulness and Aggression:

- These feline behaviors can mirror our own suppressed anger or frustration.
- Observe how you react to your cat's playfulness. Do you feel a surge of competitiveness or a desire to control the situation?
- These reactions might be clues about your own shadow self.

Independence and Detachment:

- Cats fiercely guard their autonomy.
- Does your cat's aloofness trigger feelings of insecurity or abandonment?
- These reactions might be pointing towards a shadow aspect related to attachment or codependency.

Cleanliness Instincts:

- Cats are meticulous groomers.
- Do you find yourself overly critical of yourself or others in your pursuit of perfection?
- This might be a shadow manifestation related to control or judgment.

Techniques for Shadow Work with Your Cat:

Shadow Meditation with Your Cat:

1. Sit comfortably with your cat nearby.
2. Close your eyes and visualize a dark cave or hidden chamber within your psyche.
3. Imagine your cat acting out a specific shadow trait you'd like to explore (e.g., playful aggression).
4. Observe your emotional and physical reactions. Is there fear, anger, or a sense of amusement? These reactions offer clues about your shadow self. After a while, gently open your eyes and spend time with your cat, acknowledging their presence and the messages they've brought to light.
5. **Journaling After Shadow Work Encounters:** Record your experiences with your cat, your emotional reactions, and any insights you gained about your shadow self. Over time, journaling can reveal patterns and help you integrate these shadow aspects into a more whole and authentic self.

Challenges and Considerations:

- **Not All Cats are Shadow Work Champions:** Some cats, particularly shy or anxious felines, might not be comfortable participating in shadow work rituals. Respect your cat's boundaries and choose another time or technique if they seem stressed.
- **Shadow Work Can Be Uncomfortable:** Facing your shadow can be emotionally challenging. Be gentle with yourself and take breaks when needed. If shadow work feels overwhelming, consider seeking guidance from a therapist or experienced witch.

Integrating Your Shadow with Feline Wisdom:

- By working with your cat in shadow work, you can gain valuable insights into your hidden aspects and begin to integrate them into your whole self.
- Your cat acts as a guide, challenging you to confront repressed emotions and embrace your inner wildness.
- Just like a playful swat can turn into a loving purr, shadow work can ultimately lead to self-acceptance and a deeper connection with your authentic self, and with your feline familiar.

Remember, shadow work is a journey, not a destination. By working with your cat and embracing the wisdom they offer, you can transform your shadow into a source of strength, creativity, and personal growth.

Part 5: Appendix

Glossary: Feline Familiars and the Witch's Craft

This glossary defines key terms used throughout the book to bridge the gap between the world of cats, witchcraft, and magic.

Feline-Centric Terms:

- **Astral Travel:** The practice of consciously projecting your consciousness outside your physical body. This chapter explores the possibility of astral travel with your cat as a guide.
- **Breed Correspondences:** The idea that different cat breeds hold unique symbolic associations and energetic qualities. For example, Siamese cats might be associated with communication, while Maine Coons might represent strength and independence.

- **Catnip:** An herb that has a stimulating effect on many cats. Used ethically and sparingly, it can be incorporated into scrying rituals to enhance intuition.
- **Consecration:** A ritual act of blessing and imbuing an object with magical energy. This can be done with your cat's toys, climbing structures, or your altar space.
- **Divination:** The art of using various methods to gain insights into the past, present, or future. This chapter explores techniques of cat-inspired divination, interpreting feline behavior, and using catnip as a scrying aid.
- **Energy:** A subtle force believed to permeate all living things and the environment. Witches often work by manipulating and directing energy for magical purposes.
- **Familiar:** In witchcraft traditions, a familiar is a spirit companion that offers guidance and assistance. This chapter explores the concept of a familiar embodied by a cat, either physically or as a magical construct.
- **Intention:** A focused mental state directed toward a specific goal or outcome. Setting clear intentions is crucial in all magical practices, including those involving your feline familiar.
- **Ritual:** A set of symbolic actions performed for a specific purpose. Witches use rituals for consecration, divination, and other magical workings.
- **Scrying:** A form of divination that involves gazing into a reflective surface, such as a crystal ball or water, to receive insights. This chapter explores using catnip as a scrying aid.
- **Sigil:** A symbolic representation, often geometric in design, imbued with magical intent. This chapter explores creating a sigil to represent a feline familiar.
- **Thoughtform:** A non-physical energetic construct created and sustained through focused intention and visualization. This chapter explores creating a thought form familiar in the essence of a cat.

This glossary provides a starting point for understanding the key terms used in this book. As you dive deeper into the world of feline familiars and witchcraft, you'll encounter a wealth of additional terminology. Embrace the journey of exploration, and allow the magic of cats to guide you on your path.

Bibliography: A Journey Beyond the Paw Prints

Cats and Their Magical Nature:

- **Cat vs. Man: The Perpetual Conflict by Cleveland Amory:** A humorous and insightful exploration of the historical relationship between humans and cats, offering a glimpse into the feline mystique.
- **The Encyclopedia of Magical Creatures: Mythical Beasts and Folklore by Rosemary Ellen Guiley:** This comprehensive reference explores the symbolism and magical associations of cats across various cultures.

- **The Secret Language of Cats by Carole Wilkinson:** A guide to understanding feline behavior and communication, helping you decipher your cat's subtle cues.

Witchcraft and Feline Familiars:

- **Crafting Spells: An Introduction to Making Magic by Kathryn Soanes:** A practical guide to creating and casting spells, offering inspiration for incorporating feline energy into your magical workings.
- **The Familiars of Witches by Elaine Morgan:** Delves into the history and mythology of familiars in witchcraft traditions, offering insights into the unique bond between witch and familiar.
- **The Witching Way of Herbal Magic by Phyllis Curott:** Explores the use of herbs in magic, including those with calming or stimulating properties for cats, ethically used in your practice.

Feng Shui for Harmony:

- **The Feng Shui Handbook by Eva Wong:** A comprehensive guide to the principles of Feng Shui, offering practical tips for creating a harmonious and balanced living space.
- **The Secret Language of Your Home by Karen McMillan:** Examines how the arrangement of your home can impact your well-being, offering Feng Shui techniques to create a space that supports your magical practice.
- **The Tao of Cats: Ancient Wisdom for Feline Companions by Mieshelle DeJong:** Explores the connection between cats and Taoist principles, offering guidance on creating a peaceful environment for both you and your cat.

Additional Resources:

- Websites dedicated to cat behavior and communication. (Listed below)
- Online communities focused on feline witchcraft and magical practices.
- Local metaphysical shops and libraries may offer resources on witchcraft, Feng Shui, and animal symbolism.

Remember, this bibliography is just a starting point. As you explore further, trust your intuition and seek out resources that resonate with you and your feline companion. Happy reading, and may your journey be filled with purrs and magic!

Websites Dedicated to Cat Behavior and Communication:

- **The American Society for the Prevention of Cruelty to Animals (ASPCA) (https://www.aspca.org/):** Offers a wealth of resources on cat care, behavior, and training.
- **The International Association of Animal Behavior Consultants (https://iaabc.org/):** Provides information on finding certified animal behavior consultants who can help with specific cat behavior challenges.
- **The Cat Language Translator (https://www.jacksongalaxy.com/):** Offers resources and courses on understanding feline body language and communication.

Websites Devoted to Cat Magic or Education About It:

- **CatSynth (https://www.witchesmassbay.com/events/cats-magic-the-feline-in-witchcraft-folklore-and-myth/):** Explores various magical practices, including some that incorporate cats and feline symbolism.
- **The Traveling Witch (https://thetravelingwitch.com/):** Provides resources and information on various witchcraft traditions, some of which touch upon the role of cats in magic.

Disclaimer: It's important to note that cat magic, as a specific practice, is not a mainstream school of witchcraft. These websites represent a small sampling of resources available online, and it's always wise to approach any information with a critical eye and ensure it aligns with your own ethical practices and beliefs.

As you turn the final page, a sense of accomplishment washes over you. You've not only unlocked the secrets of cat communication but also discovered the true magic that lies within this extraordinary partnership. Gazing at your purring companion curled up beside you, a newfound respect and understanding bloom in your heart. You know, with absolute certainty, that the journey you've embarked on together has just begun.

The possibilities are endless. Imagine weaving playful chases with catnip toys into elaborate rituals, or incorporating your feline friend's calming presence into meditations to amplify their focus. With each shared glance, purr, and head nudge, the bond deepens, laying the groundwork for a magical practice unlike any other. This isn't just about spells and rituals; it's about forging a connection that transcends language, enriching both your lives in ways you never thought possible. So, grab your favorite familiar, light some candles, and let the purr-powered magic begin!

www.ingramcontent.com/pod-product-compliance
Lightning Source LLC
Chambersburg PA
CBHW081155130726
47996CB00009B/3130